Contents

No. 1

¹		²			³	■	⁴	■	⁵	■	⁶

Across

1 Bob ___ : Irish singer (6)
7 Ill feeling (8)
8 Ignited (3)
9 Breakfast food (6)
10 Cook slowly in liquid (4)
11 Test or examine (5)
13 Actually; in reality (2,5)
15 Dolorous (7)
17 Doglike mammal (5)
21 Partly open (4)
22 Flat-bottomed rowing boat (6)
23 Suitable (3)
24 Material used as a colourant (8)
25 Narrow-necked bottles (6)

Down

1 Mineral of lead sulphide (6)
2 Dye used as a test of acidity (6)
3 Not true (5)
4 Reaches a destination (7)
5 Person sent on a special mission (8)
6 Meaning; purpose (6)
12 Device for spraying paint (8)
14 Fat or bulging (7)
16 Relishes (6)
18 Matches (6)
19 Lessens (6)
20 Cram (5)

No. 2

Across

1 Barely (8)
5 Sent by (4)
8 Effigies (5)
9 Confounded (7)
10 Swell with fluid (7)
12 Alan ___ : England footballer (7)
14 At the ocean floor (7)
16 Small hardy range horse (7)
18 Singer in boy band Blue (3,4)
19 Reversed (5)
20 Drains of energy (4)
21 Good-looking (8)

Down

1 Earth (4)
2 Climax or culmination (6)
3 Country in Central America (5,4)
4 Clumsy person (6)
6 Measuring sticks (6)
7 Relating to the Middle Ages (8)
11 Swift dog (9)
12 Impetus (8)
13 Not awake (6)
14 Programme; timetable (6)
15 Workplace for an artist (6)
17 Tool similar to an axe (4)

No. 3

Across

1 Raise to the third power (4)
3 Gathers together (8)
9 Large ocean (7)
10 Under (5)
11 Characteristic of the present (12)
14 Turn upside down (3)
16 Faith in another (5)
17 19th Greek letter (3)
18 Without equal (12)
21 Public square (5)
22 Friendly goodbye (7)
23 Component parts (8)
24 Clarets (4)

Down

1 Maximum number a stadium can hold (8)
2 Francis ___ : English statesman (5)
4 Mythical monster (3)
5 Scientific research rooms (12)
6 Guilty person (7)
7 Proverbs (4)
8 Loving (12)
12 Chubby (5)
13 Many (8)
15 ___ Day: Shrove Tuesday (7)
19 Long flat-bottomed boat (5)
20 Fencing sword (4)
22 Feline (3)

No. 4

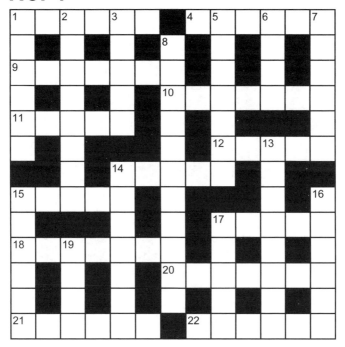

Across

1 Scratch (6)
4 Express disagreement (6)
9 Inactive pill (7)
10 Takes small bites (7)
11 Type of coffee (5)
12 Verse (5)
14 Uncovered (5)
15 Music with a recurrent theme (5)
17 Latin American dance (5)
18 Look after an infant (7)
20 Act of avoiding capture (7)
21 Stout-bodied insect (6)
22 Aircraft housing (6)

Down

1 Provide (6)
2 Response (8)
3 Portion (5)
5 Attack continuously (7)
6 Live (anag) (4)
7 Fine cloth; type of paper (6)
8 Built (11)
13 Giving way under pressure (8)
14 Augmented (7)
15 Set of instructions (6)
16 Collect or store (6)
17 Underwater breathing device (5)
19 Coalition of countries (4)

CROSSWORD

No. 5

Across

1 Resembling a hare (8)
5 Extent of a surface (4)
8 Self-evident truth (5)
9 One who assesses metals (7)
10 Hugs (7)
12 Improve (7)
14 Build in a certain place (7)
16 Coarse beach gravel (7)
18 Traditional piano keys (7)
19 Rocky; harsh (5)
20 Increase in size (4)
21 Choosing to take up or follow (8)

Down

1 Piece of foliage (4)
2 Statue base (6)
3 Staying in the same place (9)
4 Subtle variation (6)
6 Casino ___ : James Bond film (6)
7 Substance used for polishing (8)
11 Unsafe structure (9)
12 Living (8)
13 Japanese dress (6)
14 Perceived (6)
15 Long-legged rodent (6)
17 Dull car sound (4)

No. 6

CROSSWORD

Across

1 Challenge (4)
3 Fortify against attack (8)
9 Lottery (7)
10 Chairs (5)
11 Relation by marriage (7-2-3)
13 Payment for regular work (6)
15 ___ Staunton: English actress (6)
17 Awkward (12)
20 Nick ___ : Liberal Democrat politician (5)
21 Piece of furniture (7)
22 North American diving ducks (8)
23 Delighted (4)

Down

1 Structured set of information (8)
2 Lover of Juliet (5)
4 Scanty (6)
5 Lost in thought (6-6)
6 Burdensome work (7)
7 Freedom from difficulty (4)
8 First language (6,6)
12 Caught (8)
14 ___ oil: product of the flax plant (7)
16 Avoided (6)
18 Standing frame used by an artist (5)
19 Skin mark from a wound (4)

CROSSWORD

No. 7

Across

1	Helps (4)
3	Imitate (8)
9	Bad-tempered (7)
10	Strength (5)
11	Easy to converse with (12)
14	One circuit of a track (3)
16	Smallest quantity (5)
17	Circulating life force (3)
18	Productive insight (12)
21	Small farm (5)
22	Plant-eating aquatic mammal (7)
23	Light brown cane sugar (8)
24	Beers (4)

Down

1	Debatably (8)
2	Sink; sag (5)
4	Very cold; slippery (3)
5	Uncomplimentary (12)
6	Man-made fibre (7)
7	At any time (4)
8	Teacher (12)
12	Geographical plan (5)
13	International waters (4,4)
15	Carry out an action (7)
19	Up to the time when (5)
20	Corrosive substance (4)
22	Russian space station (3)

No. 8

Across

1 Glassy (8)
5 Main island of Indonesia (4)
8 Recently (5)
9 Country house (7)
10 Left out (7)
12 Throwing a coin in the air (7)
14 Pass across or through (7)
16 Painters (7)
18 Juicy soft fruit (7)
19 Wild animal; monster (5)
20 Alicia ___ : US singer (4)
21 Febrile (8)

Down

1 Climbing plant (4)
2 Tall castle structures (6)
3 Eg residents of Cairo (9)
4 Free of an obstruction (6)
6 Representatives (6)
7 Artificial water channel (8)
11 Unable to do something (9)
12 Light axe (8)
13 Level of a building (6)
14 African fly (6)
15 Sightseeing trip in Africa (6)
17 Skin irritation (4)

CROSSWORD

No. 9

Across

1 Impel (4)
3 Competitions (8)
9 Arranged neatly (7)
10 ___ firma: dry land (5)
11 Unsuitable (5)
12 Fall back (7)
13 Hatred (anag) (6)
15 Heavy food (6)
17 Newness (7)
18 Train tracks (5)
20 Part of the hand (5)
21 Form a mental picture (7)
22 Acted with hesitation (8)
23 ___ and wherefores: reasons for something (4)

Down

1 Pure (13)
2 Great sorrow (5)
4 Commands (6)
5 Dictatorial (12)
6 Marked like a zebra (7)
7 Brazenness (13)
8 Impossible to achieve (12)
14 Narrate (7)
16 Piece of text that names the writer of an article (6)
19 Nationality of Pierce Brosnan (5)

No. 10

	1	2		3		4		5		6		
7												8
				9						10		
11												
								12				
13												
								14		15		
					16	17						
18		19		20								
								21				
22				23								
	24											

Across

1 Deep regret (11)
9 The papal court (5)
10 Flightless bird (3)
11 Creep (5)
12 Stable compartment (5)
13 Acceptance of something as true (8)
16 All-round view (8)
18 Incision; indent (5)
21 Small antelope (5)
22 Chris ___ : English singer (3)
23 Condescend (5)
24 Very large city (11)

Down

2 Compels to do something (7)
3 Preserved in brine or vinegar (7)
4 Scandinavian (6)
5 Shallow food containers (5)
6 Last Greek letter (5)
7 Region including Cornwall and Devon (4,7)
8 Book issued for sale (11)
14 Capital of Ontario (7)
15 Pasta pockets (7)
17 Having colourless skin (6)
19 Historic nobleman (5)
20 Many-headed snake (5)

13

No. 11

Across

1 Turning armatures (6)
7 Relating to construction (8)
8 Thee (3)
9 Slightly annoyed (6)
10 Engrave; carve (4)
11 ___ Springfield: singer (5)
13 Dampness (7)
15 Seven-a-side game (7)
17 Skilled job (5)
21 Inflammation of an eyelid (4)
22 Sloping (of a typeface) (6)
23 Make a living with difficulty (3)
24 Female head of a town (8)
25 Young people (6)

Down

1 Had corresponding sounds (6)
2 Outdoes (6)
3 Rigid (5)
4 Sped along; skimmed (7)
5 Ruler (8)
6 Cuts up meat very finely (6)
12 Work surface (8)
14 Decimal (anag) (7)
16 Catch or snare (6)
18 Consider to be true (6)
19 Slender candles (6)
20 Common garden flower (5)

No. 12

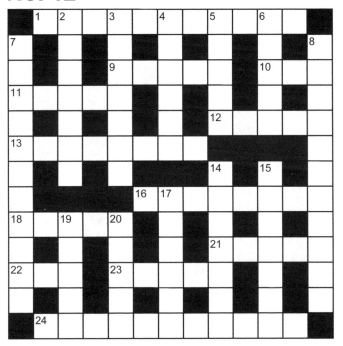

Across

1 Relation by marriage (6-2-3)
9 Ball of lead (5)
10 Longing (3)
11 Lists of restaurants dishes (5)
12 Result (5)
13 Most foolish (8)
16 Adversary (8)
18 Savour (5)
21 Make a sound expressing pain (5)
22 Fountain pen contents (3)
23 Undo (5)
24 Group of islands (11)

Down

2 Fatuously (7)
3 Nip spot (anag) (7)
4 Competition stages (6)
5 ___ gas: eg neon or argon (5)
6 Chasm (5)
7 Creating an evocative mood (11)
8 Legacy (11)
14 Curdle (7)
15 Performing a task again (7)
17 Closely held back (4-2)
19 Comedian (5)
20 Period between childhood and adulthood (5)

No. 13

Across

1 Complain unreasonably (4)
3 Changed for another (8)
9 Desist from (7)
10 Shuffles together (5)
11 Blade for rowing a boat (3)
12 Keen (5)
13 Less high (5)
15 Cook meat in the oven (5)
17 ___ acid: protein building block (5)
18 Snow runner (3)
19 Creative thoughts (5)
20 John ___ : former US tennis star (7)
21 Channels of the nose (8)
22 Dark blue colour (4)

Down

1 Confirmation (13)
2 Send someone to a medical specialist (5)
4 Glass opening in a wall (6)
5 Peruse matter (anag) (12)
6 Six-sided shape (7)
7 Devastatingly (13)
8 Troublemaker (6-6)
14 Cricket overs in which no runs are scored (7)
16 Type of living organism (6)
18 Country in Western Asia (5)

16

No. 14

Across

1 Brevity in expressing oneself (11)
9 Old-fashioned (5)
10 Trouble in mind or body (3)
11 Mosquito (5)
12 Answer (5)
13 Threatening (8)
16 Transporting by hand (8)
18 ___ Adkins: singer (5)
21 Sporting stadium (5)
22 Four-wheeled road vehicle (3)
23 Goodbye (Spanish) (5)
24 Wonderfully (11)

Down

2 Surpassed (7)
3 Musical ending (7)
4 Sixth planet from the sun (6)
5 Lowest point (5)
6 Impress a pattern on (5)
7 A recollection (11)
8 Eg Queen of Hearts (7,4)
14 Treachery (7)
15 Solid inorganic substance (7)
17 Birthplace of St Francis (6)
19 Fault; mistake (5)
20 Electronic message (5)

CROSSWORD

No. 15

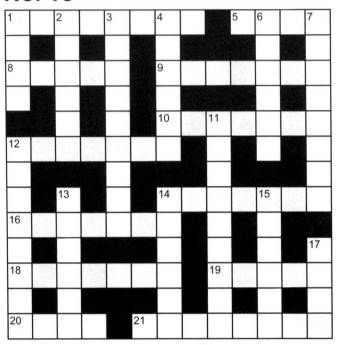

Across

1 Not absolute (8)
5 Lies (anag) (4)
8 Deprive of weapons (5)
9 Pertaining to the heart (7)
10 Makes ineffective (7)
12 Write again (7)
14 Cushions that support the head (7)
16 Admit something is true (7)
18 Preventing success; unfavourable (7)
19 Bring on oneself (5)
20 Alone (4)
21 Grotesquely carved figure (8)

Down

1 Destroy (4)
2 Laden (6)
3 Schedule (9)
4 Empty (6)
6 Evasive; devious (6)
7 Overabundances (8)
11 Running quickly (9)
12 British soldiers (historical) (8)
13 Cry and sniffle (6)
14 Former Spanish currency (6)
15 Strong public protest (6)
17 Woody perennial plant (4)

No. 16

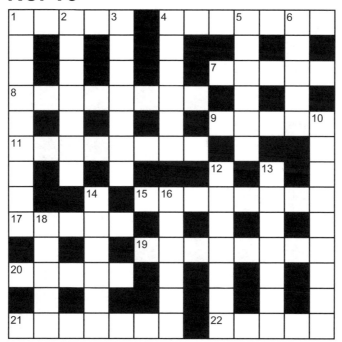

Across

1 Maladroit (5)
4 Thinning out a tree by removing branches (7)
7 Ringo ___ : one of the Beatles (5)
8 Floor covering material (8)
9 Sound (5)
11 Albert ___ : famous physicist (8)
15 Old toll road (8)
17 Flammable liquid used as an anaesthetic (5)
19 Cheeky (8)
20 Colossus (5)
21 Road or roofing material (7)
22 ___ Mirren: The Queen actress (5)

Down

1 Have an effect on another (9)
2 Distinguished (7)
3 ___ night: Shakespeare play (7)
4 Lapis ___ : blue gemstone (6)
5 Quality in speech arousing pity (6)
6 Conventions (5)
10 Amuse (9)
12 Acute suffering (7)
13 Letter-for-letter; verbatim (7)
14 Angel of the highest order (6)
16 Furthest; extreme (6)
18 Follows closely (5)

No. 17

Across

1 Scaring (11)
9 Impair (5)
10 Great distress (3)
11 Fortune-telling card (5)
12 Rope with a running noose (5)
13 Eastern (8)
16 Representations or descriptions of data (8)
18 Pulsate (5)
21 New ___ : Indian capital (5)
22 Recede (3)
23 Civilian dress (5)
24 Eg Shakespeare and Bernard Shaw (11)

Down

2 Enlist (7)
3 Acquiring (7)
4 Irrelevant pieces of information (6)
5 Relating to birth (5)
6 Amphibians (5)
7 Official bodies (11)
8 Expulsion from a country (11)
14 Marriage (7)
15 Withdraw from a commitment (4,3)
17 Bestow (6)
19 Insurgent (5)
20 Uneven (of a road surface) (5)

No. 18

Across

1 Stitching (6)
4 Academy Awards (6)
9 Quarrel (7)
10 Clergymen (7)
11 Looks slyly (5)
12 The entire scale (5)
14 Loves uncritically (5)
15 Slight error; oversight (5)
17 Measuring stick (5)
18 Standup (anag) (7)
20 Finding by investigation (7)
21 Set of steps (6)
22 Feature (6)

Down

1 Seat on the back of a horse (6)
2 Over the hill (6-2)
3 Words that identify things (5)
5 Part of an orchestra (7)
6 Increases; sums up (4)
7 Coloured evening sky (6)
8 Divisions of companies (11)
13 Eg when lunch or dinner is eaten (8)
14 Abandon hope (7)
15 Women (6)
16 Radiating light (6)
17 Calls out loudly (5)
19 Plant of the pea family (4)

No. 19

Across

1 Unwise (11)
9 ___ Arabia: country in the Middle East (5)
10 Midge ___ : Ultravox musician (3)
11 Arm joint (5)
12 Put into service (5)
13 Enter unlawfully (8)
16 Detested thing (8)
18 Wanderer (5)
21 One of the United Arab Emirates (5)
22 Head movement showing assent (3)
23 Island in the Bay of Naples (5)
24 Abashed (11)

Down

2 Tool for cutting metal (7)
3 Curved upwards (7)
4 Accustoms to something (6)
5 Island in the Mediterranean Sea (5)
6 Take the place of (5)
7 Asking (11)
8 Result of loss of water from the body (11)
14 Examines in detail (7)
15 Wordy (7)
17 Young person (6)
19 Polite address for a woman (5)
20 Russian country house (5)

No. 20

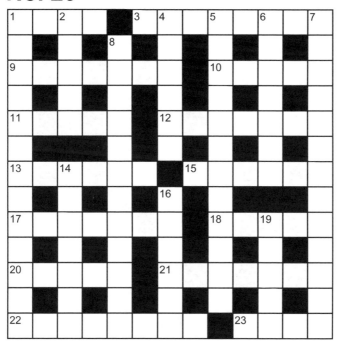

CROSSWORD

Across

1	Concern; worry (4)
3	Clear or obvious (8)
9	Remedy (7)
10	Climbing shrubs (5)
11	Eat quickly (5)
12	Movement conveying an expression (7)
13	Chat (6)
15	Exist permanently in (6)
17	Veracity (7)
18	Highways (5)
20	Join together as one (5)
21	Make less intense (7)
22	Thick dark syrup (8)
23	Scores (a goal) (4)

Down

1	Plant with bright flowers (13)
2	Wireless (5)
4	Allocate a duty (6)
5	Distinctive behavioural attribute (12)
6	Connoisseur; gourmet (7)
7	Blandness (13)
8	Altruism (12)
14	Slender stemlike plant appendage (7)
16	Revolve quickly (6)
19	Confound (5)

CROSSWORD

No. 21

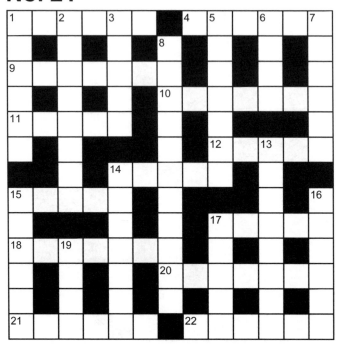

Across

1	Not sensible (6)
4	Middle Eastern language (6)
9	Gold or silver in bulk (7)
10	Bishop's jurisdiction (7)
11	Cuts slightly (5)
12	Evade (5)
14	Cooks in fat (5)
15	Japanese food (5)
17	Ironic metaphor (5)
18	Saying (7)
20	Vocabulary of a person (7)
21	Gathering up leaves in the garden (6)
22	Stage whispers (6)

Down

1	Straightened (6)
2	Exploratory oil wells (8)
3	Loses grip (5)
5	Refills (7)
6	Gareth ___ : Welsh footballer (4)
7	Dairy product (6)
8	Incapable of being split (11)
13	Separated; detached (8)
14	Male blaze fighters (7)
15	Military engineer (6)
16	Deceives; finest (anag) (6)
17	US state (5)
19	Pig noise (4)

24

No. 22

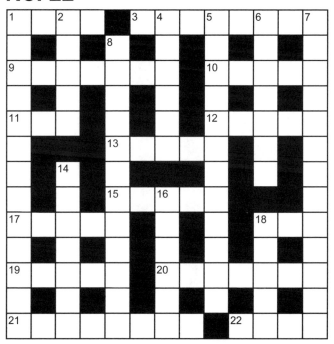

Across

1 Closing section of music (4)
3 Complying with orders (8)
9 Lead batsmen (cricket) (7)
10 Means of mass communication (5)
11 Slippery fish (3)
12 Dressed to the ___ : elaborately clothed (5)
13 British noblemen (5)
15 First Pope (5)
17 Use to one's advantage (5)
18 Cereal grass (3)
19 ___ Willoughby: TV presenter (5)
20 Unlawful (7)
21 Remaining (8)
22 Dull colour (4)

Down

1 Musical dance co-ordinator (13)
2 Reside (5)
4 More active (6)
5 Clearly evident (12)
6 Final parts of stories (7)
7 Party lanterns (anag) (13)
8 Working for oneself (4-8)
14 Buildings for horses (7)
16 Russian carriage (6)
18 Happen again (5)

CROSSWORD

No. 23

Across

1	Sort (4)
3	Rubbish (8)
9	Novice driver (7)
10	Senior figure in a tribe (5)
11	Large deer (5)
12	Ugly building (7)
13	Material wealth (6)
15	Out of breath (6)
17	South American country (7)
18	Savoury meat jelly (5)
20	Henrik ___ : Norwegian dramatist (5)
21	Not level (7)
22	Horticulturist (8)
23	Dam (4)

Down

1	Advertising by telephone (13)
2	Musical instrument (5)
4	Pantry (6)
5	Planned in advance (12)
6	Huge coniferous tree (7)
7	Upright; vertical (13)
8	Freedom from control (12)
14	Warship (7)
16	Game bird; grumble (6)
19	Cut back a tree (5)

No. 24

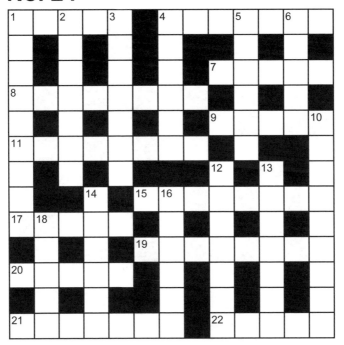

Across

1 Hunt (5)
4 Short trips (7)
7 Make a search (5)
8 Game of chance (8)
9 Applauds (5)
11 Unselfish concern for others (8)
15 Wild flower (8)
17 Conceals (5)
19 Judges; evaluates (8)
20 Lukewarm (5)
21 Eg Iceland and Borneo (7)
22 Harsh and serious in manner (5)

Down

1 Male head of a family (9)
2 Motivate (7)
3 Feeling positive (7)
4 Ice shoes (6)
5 Excite agreeably (6)
6 Supply with; furnish (5)
10 Isolation (9)
12 Old Spanish currency (pl) (7)
13 Express severe disapproval of (7)
14 Part of the eye (6)
16 Opposite of winners (6)
18 Individual things (5)

No. 25

Across

1 Lavish (8)
5 Chief god of ancient Greece (4)
8 Fruit of the oak (5)
9 Public transport vehicle (7)
10 Avoidance (7)
12 Varnish (7)
14 Ancient Egyptian ruler (7)
16 Arguer (7)
18 Efficiency (7)
19 Cuban folk dance (5)
20 Cries (4)
21 Visionary; utopian (8)

Down

1 Mountain top (4)
2 Humorously sarcastic (6)
3 Flowing together (9)
4 Rubbish (6)
6 Greek mathematician (6)
7 Physical power (8)
11 Ridge of the Himalayas (9)
12 Magnitude of a sound (8)
13 Soak up (6)
14 Made a victim of (6)
15 Graduates of an academic institution (6)
17 Adult male deer (4)

No. 26

Across

1 Highest point (4)
3 Altruistic (8)
9 Bacterium (7)
10 Strain (5)
11 Approaches (5)
12 Snared (7)
13 Residential district (6)
15 Ukrainian port (6)
17 Use again (7)
18 Established custom (5)
20 Musical speeds (5)
21 Planet (7)
22 Left one's job (8)
23 ___ Ifans: Welsh actor (4)

Down

1 Person performing official duties (13)
2 Type of coffee drink (5)
4 Constructs (6)
5 Popular takeaway food (4,3,5)
6 Frees from an obligation (7)
7 Loyalty in the face of trouble (13)
8 Building (12)
14 Suits; turns into (7)
16 Close-fitting hat (6)
19 Redden (5)

CROSSWORD

No. 27

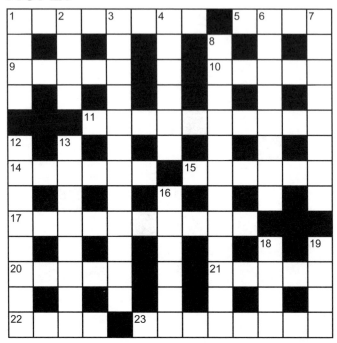

Across

1 Trails alongside canals (8)
5 Dutch cheese (4)
9 Eg the Thames (5)
10 Borders (5)
11 Overawe (10)
14 Melodious (6)
15 Venomous snakes (6)
17 Descriptive account (10)
20 Bird sound (5)
21 Ahead of time (5)
22 Portion of medicine (4)
23 A canine (3,5)

Down

1 Fruit pie (4)
2 Slightly curling lock of hair (4)
3 Agreements; plans (12)
4 Excessive self-confidence (6)
6 In poor condition (3-5)
7 Uses seam (anag) (8)
8 Total confusion (12)
12 Taught (8)
13 Mountaineers (8)
16 Not moving or shaking (6)
18 Group of three (4)
19 Legendary story (4)

No. 28

Across

1 Recording medium (4)
3 Deceive (8)
9 Furthest away (7)
10 Sweetener (5)
11 Easy-going (4-8)
14 Pull at (3)
16 Bond or connection (5)
17 Intentionally so written (3)
18 Ineptness (12)
21 Double-reed instruments (5)
22 Mass of flowers (7)
23 Broad and strongly built (8)
24 Lids (anag) (4)

Down

1 Ideas (8)
2 Paved courtyard (5)
4 Widely cultivated cereal grass (3)
5 Exemption from a rule (12)
6 Act of entering (7)
7 Pavement edge (4)
8 Endlessly (12)
12 Confusion (3-2)
13 Shouted very loudly (8)
15 Venetian boat (7)
19 Of the nose (5)
20 ___ Hartnett: actor (4)
22 Insect which collects pollen (3)

31

No. 29

Across

1 Shameful (11)
9 Type of chemical bond (5)
10 Young dog (3)
11 Type of primula (5)
12 Pertaining to the moon (5)
13 Lower (8)
16 Distinguishing mark (8)
18 Rapidity of movement (5)
21 Excuse of any kind (5)
22 Unit of energy (3)
23 Broom made of twigs (5)
24 Stood for (11)

Down

2 Slanted characters (7)
3 Held tightly (7)
4 Declares invalid (6)
5 Do extremely well at (5)
6 Unfasten a garment (5)
7 Company that transmits TV shows (11)
8 Praise (11)
14 Organic nutrient (7)
15 Ennoble (7)
17 Hospital carers (6)
19 A score of two under par on a hole (golf) (5)
20 Suspend; prevent (5)

No. 30

Across

1	Alluring (8)
5	Travelled too quickly (4)
8	African country (5)
9	Root vegetables (7)
10	Reprimand (7)
12	Grapple with (7)
14	Creatures (7)
16	Car motors (7)
18	Set apart (7)
19	Tines (anag) (5)
20	Deities (4)
21	Padding (8)

Down

1	Capture a piece in chess (4)
2	Sleeveless cloak (6)
3	Custom (9)
4	Character of a person (6)
6	Place of confinement (6)
7	Sweet food courses (8)
11	Person bringing a legal case (9)
12	Broadening (8)
13	Ancient or well established (3-3)
14	Agreement (6)
15	Andre ___ : tennis player (6)
17	Male deer (4)

CROSSWORD

No. 31

Across

1. Knocks into (5)
4. Working extremely hard (7)
7. Covered with water (5)
8. Stumbling (8)
9. Belief in a god or gods (5)
11. Monarchist (8)
15. Able to adjust (8)
17. Produce as a fruit (5)
19. Overflowing with praise (8)
20. Utter impulsively (5)
21. Rinsed around (7)
22. Mournful song (5)

Down

1. Colourful insect (9)
2. ___ Monroe: famous actress (7)
3. Shoulder blade (7)
4. Strong ringing sounds (6)
5. Solicitor (6)
6. Birds lay their eggs in these (5)
10. Be coherent (4,5)
12. Smartened up (7)
13. Prophet (7)
14. Not singular (6)
16. Guard against (6)
18. Relation by marriage (2-3)

No. 32

Across

1 Purchases (4)
3 Central American monkey (8)
9 Salad vegetable (7)
10 Warning noise (5)
11 What p.m. stands for (4,8)
14 Mock (3)
16 Closely compacted (5)
17 Born (3)
18 Jail term without end (4,8)
21 ___ du Beke: ballroom dancer (5)
22 Oppressive rulers (7)
23 Type of melon (8)
24 Low dull sound (4)

Down

1 Approximate (of a price) (8)
2 Abominable snowmen (5)
4 Metric unit of measurement (historical) (3)
5 Mishap (12)
6 Operating doctor (7)
7 Melody (4)
8 Brusque and surly (12)
12 Wash in water to remove soap or dirt (5)
13 Moved backwards (8)
15 Inherent (of a characteristic) (5-2)
19 Between eighth and tenth (5)
20 Whip (4)
22 Definite article (3)

No. 33

Across

1 Courteous (6)
7 Barely adequate (8)
8 Mist (3)
9 Listener (6)
10 International exhibition (4)
11 Cleans (5)
13 With a look of suspicion (7)
15 ___ of the Opera: musical (7)
17 Church council (5)
21 Greek god of war (4)
22 A complex whole (6)
23 Short cylindrical piece of wood (3)
24 Simple and unsophisticated (8)
25 Mel ___ : Braveheart actor (6)

Down

1 Breathless (6)
2 Devices that illuminate (6)
3 Coarse rock used for polishing (5)
4 Speech; where you live (7)
5 Culinary herb (8)
6 Line of latitude (6)
12 Metallic element (8)
14 Spreads rumours (7)
16 Agricultural implement (6)
18 Insect larvae (6)
19 Fire-breathing monster (6)
20 Employing (5)

No. 34

Across

1 Representation of a person (6)
4 Special ___ : film illusion (6)
9 Qualification attached to a statement (7)
10 Loud and hoarse (7)
11 Assesses performance (5)
12 Sorts (5)
14 Irritate (5)
15 Enclosed (of animals) (5)
17 Japanese poem (5)
18 Highest singing voice (7)
20 Coming first (7)
21 Varied mixture of things (6)
22 Liveliness (6)

Down

1 Domain (6)
2 Moving on the surface of water (8)
3 Grasps tightly (5)
5 Talent for doing something (7)
6 Therefore (Latin) (4)
7 Has confidence in (6)
8 Former Labour Prime Minister (6,5)
13 Peacemaker (8)
14 Go forward (7)
15 Tradition (6)
16 Gold lump (6)
17 Suspends (5)
19 Push; poke (4)

No. 35

Across

1 Long walk (4)
3 Unfit for consumption (of food) (8)
9 Egg white (7)
10 Small loose stones (5)
11 Awkward (12)
14 Remove branches (3)
16 Venomous snake (5)
17 Foot extremity (3)
18 Corresponding; proportionate (12)
21 Very pale (5)
22 Temperature scale (7)
23 Blue toys (anag) (8)
24 Clutched (4)

Down

1 Blissful (8)
2 Skewered meat (5)
4 Religious sister (3)
5 Ruinously (12)
6 Hereditary title (7)
7 Days before major events (4)
8 Enhancements (12)
12 Trembling poplar (5)
13 Set free (8)
15 Soothsayer (7)
19 Not dead (5)
20 Light circle around the head of a saint (4)
22 Mountain pass (3)

No. 36

Across

1 Correct (5)
4 Farewell remark (7)
7 Pulpy (5)
8 Motionless (8)
9 Greek writer of fables (5)
11 Inclination (8)
15 Daydreamer (8)
17 Titled (5)
19 Very attractive (of personality) (8)
20 Town in Surrey; sheer (anag) (5)
21 Cowboy hat (7)
22 Prohibited by social custom (5)

Down

1 Divergence out from a central point (9)
2 Item of clothing (7)
3 Fell over (7)
4 Characteristically French (6)
5 Extinguished (6)
6 Loutish person (5)
10 Nut (9)
12 Sincere (7)
13 Move something; agitate (7)
14 Feel sorrow for one's deeds (6)
16 Clean-___ : without a beard (6)
18 Item of value (5)

No. 37

Across

1 Type of social occasion (6,5)
9 Natural elevation (5)
10 In favour of (3)
11 Person who steals (5)
12 Implied without being stated (5)
13 Ruler (8)
16 Concurring (8)
18 Animal enclosures (5)
21 Apply pressure (5)
22 Short sleep (3)
23 Synthetic fabric (5)
24 Serving to enlighten; instructive (11)

Down

2 Inner parts of things (7)
3 English county (7)
4 Steering mechanism of a boat (6)
5 Representative (5)
6 Theme for a discussion (5)
7 Bringing into use (11)
8 Every two weeks (11)
14 Film starring Guy Pearce (7)
15 Country in West Africa (7)
17 Throat (6)
19 Looked at open-mouthed (5)
20 Pertaining to sound (5)

No. 38

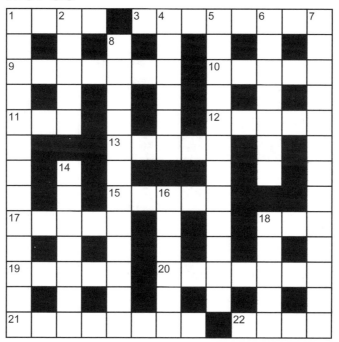

Across

1 Place for a drink or light meal (4)
3 Progresses (8)
9 Attains (7)
10 Tremulous sound (5)
11 Boolean operator (3)
12 Unit of weight (5)
13 ___ days: long ago (5)
15 Darkness (5)
17 Chart (5)
18 Be in debt (3)
19 Punctuation mark (5)
20 Group of four (7)
21 Diminished (8)
22 Having pains (4)

Down

1 Arranged in temporal order (13)
2 Stylishness and originality (5)
4 Removed dirt from (6)
5 Extremely large (12)
6 Sophisticated hair style (7)
7 Obviously (4-9)
8 Street (12)
14 Ionised gases (7)
16 Not allowing light to pass through (6)
18 Relating to vision (5)

41

CROSSWORD

No. 39

Across

1 Gear wheels (4)
3 Soft leather shoe (8)
9 Extract (7)
10 Conveyed by gestures (5)
11 Large Brazilian city (3,2,7)
13 Wear away (6)
15 One's environment (6)
17 Quality of being at hand when necessary (12)
20 Corpulent (5)
21 Important church (7)
22 Scantily (8)
23 Memo (4)

Down

1 Road you cannot stop on (8)
2 Type of lizard (5)
4 Expenditure (6)
5 Contests (12)
6 Japanese warrior (7)
7 Dons (anag) (4)
8 Amiability (12)
12 Exempt from tax (4-4)
14 Mediterranean coastal region (7)
16 Eg monkey or whale (6)
18 Prologue (abbrev) (5)
19 Gardening tools used for weeding (4)

No. 40

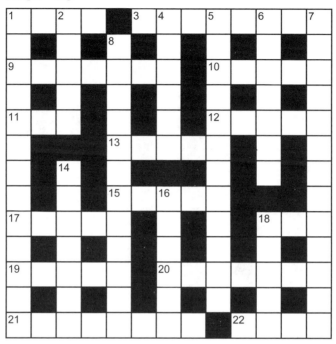

Across

1 Passage (4)
3 Of great value (8)
9 Reversing something (7)
10 Mother-of-pearl (5)
11 Brett ___ : Australian fast bowler (3)
12 Draw or bring out (5)
13 ___ Nash: writer of light verse (5)
15 Sign of the zodiac (5)
17 All (5)
18 Policeman (3)
19 Sailing ship (5)
20 Costing (anag) (7)
21 Flooded (8)
22 By word of mouth (4)

Down

1 Verified for a second time (6-7)
2 Core group; basic unit (5)
4 Tattered (6)
5 Reverse of vaporisation (12)
6 Block (7)
7 Lacking originality (13)
8 Written in pictorial symbols (12)
14 Playhouse (7)
16 Bracelet (6)
18 Supply with food (5)

43

No. 41

Across

1 Be aggrieved by (6)
4 Part of a tree (6)
9 Uma ___ : US actress (7)
10 Excited agreeably (7)
11 Compass point (5)
12 Substance exuded by some trees (5)
14 Judged; ranked (5)
15 The reproduction of sound (5)
17 Indian rice dish (5)
18 Kitchen (anag) (7)
20 Process of wearing away (7)
21 Fatty matter (6)
22 Measurement of extent (6)

Down

1 Plump (6)
2 Emitted a jet of liquid (8)
3 Insect larva (5)
5 Parachute opener (7)
6 Invalid; void (4)
7 Involving direct confrontation (4-2)
8 Amused (11)
13 Dropping a catch (in ball games) (8)
14 Projectile fireworks (7)
15 Performing on stage (6)
16 Extinguish (a fire) (6)
17 Explore or examine (5)
19 Paul ___ : former England footballer (4)

44

No. 42

Across

1 Widespread (4)
3 Sharply defined (5-3)
9 Mythical bird (7)
10 Stage play (5)
11 Long essay (12)
14 Your (poetic) (3)
16 Underground railway (5)
17 Increase the running speed of an engine (3)
18 Heavy long-handled tool (12)
21 ___ Lewis: British singer (5)
22 Cornmeal (7)
23 Informal term for a feline pet (8)
24 Curved shapes (4)

Down

1 Swiftness (8)
2 Deceives (5)
4 Negligent (3)
5 And also (12)
6 Loud outcry (7)
7 Tailless amphibian (4)
8 Middleman (12)
12 Name of a book (5)
13 Bridge above another road (8)
15 Eg primrose and lemon (7)
19 Lesser (5)
20 Turn over (4)
22 Small legume (3)

CROSSWORD

No. 43

Across

1 Torso (4)
3 Strongholds (8)
9 Yields a supply of (7)
10 Clergyman (5)
11 Climbing plant (3)
12 ___ Jones: American singer-songwriter (5)
13 Turn inside out (5)
15 Happening (5)
17 Land measures (5)
18 Pear-shaped fruit (3)
19 US state (5)
20 Former student (7)
21 Someone with the same moniker (8)
22 Energy and enthusiasm (4)

Down

1 Step towards canonisation (13)
2 Silly (5)
4 Instep (6)
5 Coming from outside (12)
6 Bodyguards (7)
7 The Duchess of York (5,8)
8 Ancestors (12)
14 Type of humour (7)
16 Set out on a journey (6)
18 Ultimate (5)

No. 44

Across

1 Blinking like a light (8)
5 Falls back (4)
8 Samantha ___ : Irish singer (5)
9 Quiver (7)
10 Bewitch (7)
12 Swam like a dog (7)
14 Predatory fish (7)
16 Part of the ocean (4,3)
18 Violent troublemakers (7)
19 Snow home (5)
20 24-hour periods (4)
21 Recognise (8)

Down

1 Renown (4)
2 Nut-like seed that marzipan is made from (6)
3 Unfeeling (9)
4 Tented (anag) (6)
6 Small N American lynx (6)
7 Flowering plant (5,3)
11 Rust (9)
12 Consisting of fine particles (8)
13 Recollection (6)
14 Stopped temporarily (6)
15 Central parts of cells (6)
17 Drowsy (4)

47

No. 45

Across

1 Edible tuber (6)
7 Thoroughly conversant with (8)
8 Opposite of no (3)
9 Pilfers (6)
10 Form of rock music (4)
11 ___ Izzard: English stand-up comedian (5)
13 Go backwards (7)
15 Part of a gun (7)
17 Computer memory units (5)
21 Potential applications (4)
22 Reprimand (6)
23 Limb used for walking (3)
24 Get ready for a later performance (8)
25 Feels upset and annoyed (6)

Down

1 Soul; spirit (6)
2 Flipped a coin (6)
3 Bits of meat of low value (5)
4 Broke into pieces (7)
5 Unreliable; shifty (8)
6 Gives a description of (6)
12 Took in (8)
14 Coatings (7)
16 Duster (anag) (6)
18 Bank employee (6)
19 Raised theatre platforms (6)
20 Zodiac sign (5)

No. 46

Across

1 At a distance (4)
3 Teacher (8)
9 Acted properly (7)
10 Supply with new weapons (5)
11 Sea duck (5)
12 Boastful person (7)
13 Money received (6)
15 Calamitous (6)
17 Binned (7)
18 Hymn of thanksgiving (5)
20 Expels from a position (5)
21 Electric appliance (7)
22 Ominous (8)
23 Effigy (4)

Down

1 Shortened forms of words (13)
2 Small plant-sucking insect (5)
4 Evades (6)
5 Mapmaker (12)
6 Melting (7)
7 Device for changing TV channel (6,7)
8 Excessive stress (12)
14 Corneas (anag) (7)
16 Fit for consumption (6)
19 Finished (5)

CROSSWORD

No. 47

Across

1 Pierce with a horn (4)
3 African country (8)
9 Loud enough to be heard (7)
10 Sells (5)
11 Terrified or extremely shocked (6-6)
13 Exclusive circle of people (6)
15 Come off the tracks (6)
17 Small garden carts (12)
20 Diacritical mark (5)
21 Baltic country (7)
22 Organism that exploits another (8)
23 Indolently (4)

Down

1 Diagrams (8)
2 Detection technology (5)
4 Tithes (anag) (6)
5 Animal lacking a backbone (12)
6 Remedy for everything (7)
7 Too; in addition (4)
8 Completeness (12)
12 Alphabetical list of terms (8)
14 Item used by asthma sufferers (7)
16 Not present (6)
18 Possessed (5)
19 Pace (4)

No. 48

Across

1 Spies (8)
5 Part of the eye (4)
9 Lance (5)
10 Antelope (5)
11 Culmination (10)
14 Suggestion (6)
15 Smear or blur (6)
17 Discretion (anag) (10)
20 Respond to (5)
21 Surround and harass (5)
22 Move like a wheel (4)
23 Space rock (8)

Down

1 Breathe convulsively (4)
2 Individual article or unit (4)
3 Shrewdness (12)
4 Next after seventh (6)
6 Strip of land by a highway (8)
7 Move out the way of (8)
8 Resolvable (12)
12 Person walking aimlessly (8)
13 Take to pieces to examine (8)
16 Locks lips with (6)
18 Capital of Norway (4)
19 Metal fastener (4)

No. 49

Across

1 Takes an exam (4)
3 Starchy edible tubers (8)
9 Coincide partially (7)
10 Large and cumbersome (5)
11 Exceptional (12)
13 Give formal consent to (6)
15 Reveal (6)
17 Place of conflict (12)
20 Christina ___ : actress (5)
21 Complain; moan (7)
22 Coming into view (8)
23 Taxis (4)

Down

1 Two-wheeled vehicles (8)
2 Eighth Greek letter (5)
4 Fish-eating bird of prey (6)
5 Able to use both hands well (12)
6 ___ Bloom: English actor (7)
7 Island of the Inner Hebrides (4)
8 Tight (of clothing) (5-7)
12 Unnecessary (8)
14 Share; portion (7)
16 Ronald ___ : former US President (6)
18 Shadow (5)
19 At liberty (4)

No. 50

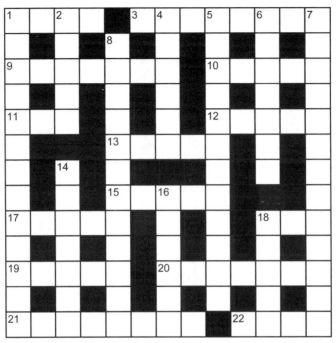

Across

1 Strain (4)
3 Unclean (8)
9 Readable (7)
10 Mashes (5)
11 Very long period of time (3)
12 Gardening tool (5)
13 Meal (5)
15 Locomotive (5)
17 Flaring stars (5)
18 Lout (3)
19 Male relation (5)
20 Newtlike salamander (7)
21 Inclined (8)
22 Openly refuse to obey an order (4)

Down

1 Eloquent; articulate (6-7)
2 Character in Oliver Twist (5)
4 Liam ___ : Schindler's List actor (6)
5 Foreboding (12)
6 Eg fluorine or chlorine (7)
7 Suspiciously (13)
8 Lowest possible temperature (8,4)
14 Gadgets (7)
16 Mysterious; secret (6)
18 Form of oxygen found in the atmosphere (5)

CROSSWORD

No. 51

Across

1 Brawny (8)
5 Mix; agitate (4)
9 Coming after (5)
10 Leases (5)
11 Unbiased and just (4-6)
14 Ticket (6)
15 Reach a specified level (6)
17 How something looks (10)
20 Aromatic herb (5)
21 ___ Halfpenny: rugby player (5)
22 Finishes (4)
23 Speaking many languages (8)

Down

1 Where one finds Bamako (4)
2 Badger's home (4)
3 Not guided by good sense (12)
4 Major blood vessel (6)
6 Unable to appreciate music (4-4)
7 Living in (8)
8 In a creative manner (12)
12 Clamber (8)
13 Assumed (8)
16 Small garden building (6)
18 Tablet (4)
19 Hots (anag) (4)

54

No. 52

Across

1 Clenched hands (5)
4 Eg ape or human (7)
7 Willow twig (5)
8 A formal exposition (8)
9 Fop (5)
11 Remove from action (8)
15 Evaluator (8)
17 Small container (5)
19 Coloured paper thrown at weddings (8)
20 Backless sofa (5)
21 Broke free from confinement (7)
22 Prophets (5)

Down

1 Excellent (9)
2 Long speeches (7)
3 Coal bucket (7)
4 Rector or vicar (6)
5 Misplace (6)
6 Thick woollen fabric (5)
10 Desires (9)
12 Cows (7)
13 Form of an element (7)
14 US state (6)
16 Displayed (6)
18 Attacks without warning (5)

No. 53

Across

1 Keep secret (4,2)
7 Elation (8)
8 Long deep track (3)
9 Frederic ___ : Polish composer (6)
10 Appendage (4)
11 Meads (anag) (5)
13 Gives up one's job (7)
15 Leave quickly and in secret (7)
17 Doctor (5)
21 Hit with a lash (4)
22 Excessively bright (6)
23 Bottle top (3)
24 Giant ocean waves (8)
25 Breathe out (6)

Down

1 Rounded up animals (6)
2 Humorous television drama (6)
3 Looks furtively (5)
4 Small wood (7)
5 Bring about using artifice (8)
6 Relating to monkeys (6)
12 Getting away from (8)
14 Final stage of a process (7)
16 Bidding (6)
18 Plant of the daisy family (6)
19 One who carries golf clubs (6)
20 Rub out (5)

No. 54

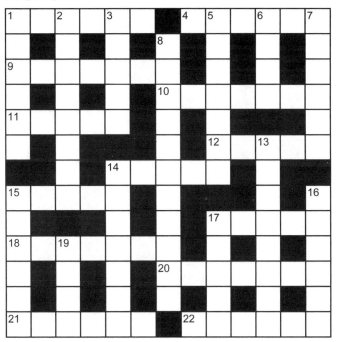

Across

1 Provoke (6)
4 Increase in intensity (4,2)
9 Cause to taste more sugary (7)
10 Considerate; diplomatic (7)
11 Rugby formation (5)
12 City in Tuscany (5)
14 Pale brownish-yellow colour (5)
15 Sweet-scented shrub (5)
17 Longest river in Europe (5)
18 Give in to temptation (7)
20 Foes (7)
21 Discontinuance (6)
22 Book of the Bible (6)

Down

1 Take a firm stand (6)
2 In good spirits (8)
3 ___ pole: tribal emblem (5)
5 Dribble (7)
6 Light blast of wind (4)
7 Spanish rice dish (6)
8 Small room that leads to a main one (11)
13 Immature (8)
14 Conceals something from view (7)
15 Itemised (6)
16 Title of Roman emperors (6)
17 Changes direction suddenly (5)
19 Domestic felines (4)

No. 55

Across

1 Wine container (4)
3 Reading quickly (8)
9 Small Arctic whale (7)
10 Capital of Japan (5)
11 Fat-like compound (5)
12 Eg anger or love (7)
13 Protects (6)
15 Failed to remember (6)
17 Upward slopes (7)
18 Lazy person (5)
20 ___ Milan: football team (5)
21 Demanded (7)
22 Pleasantness (8)
23 Tax (4)

Down

1 Intense fire (13)
2 Device used to sharpen razors (5)
4 Out of ___ : not in harmony (6)
5 Based on legend (12)
6 Vague understanding; hint (7)
7 Amiably (4-9)
8 Evergreen shrub (12)
14 Person who practises self-discipline (7)
16 Organic compounds (6)
19 Metric unit of capacity (5)

No. 56

Across

1 Component parts (11)
9 ___ Valletta: Hitch actress (5)
10 Antelope (3)
11 Grade (anag) (5)
12 Badgers' homes (5)
13 Liking for something (8)
16 Point of contact; masonry support (8)
18 Opposite of lows (5)
21 Surprise result (5)
22 Propel a boat (3)
23 Mike ___ : US boxer (5)
24 Amazing (11)

Down

2 Pestering constantly (7)
3 Town in Berkshire (7)
4 Suspends; prevents (6)
5 Acquires through merit (5)
6 Taut (5)
7 Ancestors (11)
8 Replaced with another (11)
14 Steadfast (7)
15 Mental strain (7)
17 Dwarfed tree (6)
19 Loose garments (5)
20 Fight (3-2)

CROSSWORD

No. 57

Across

1. Type of starch (4)
3. Partially hidden (8)
9. Flotation device in water (7)
10. Brilliant and clear (5)
11. Deceitfully (12)
14. Carry a heavy object (3)
16. Throw forcefully (5)
17. Consume food (3)
18. One who takes part in a protest (12)
21. Common greeting (5)
22. Break between words (in verse) (7)
23. Financially ruined (8)
24. Ewer (anag) (4)

Down

1. Raised wooden platform (8)
2. Third Greek letter (5)
4. Auction offer (3)
5. Popular district in London (6,6)
6. Rotate (7)
7. Part of a pedestal (4)
8. Bride's primary attendant (4,2,6)
12. Dens (5)
13. Study the night sky (8)
15. Imaginary mischievous sprite (7)
19. Armistice (5)
20. Freshwater game fish (4)
22. Container for a drink (3)

No. 58

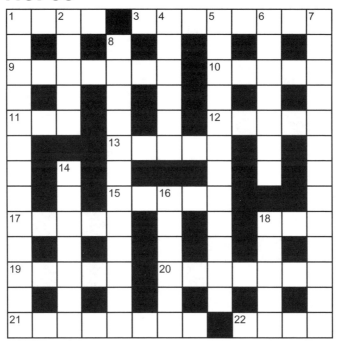

Across

1 Plant containers (4)
3 Grammatical case (8)
9 Tool for the Arctic (3,4)
10 Inexpensive (5)
11 What painters create (3)
12 Gain knowledge (5)
13 Completely; really (5)
15 Major artery (5)
17 Wanderer (5)
18 Chopping tool (3)
19 Position carefully (5)
20 Passionate (7)
21 Wood preserver (8)
22 Bonus; positive (4)

Down

1 Benevolent and generous (13)
2 Act of stealing (5)
4 Swimming costume (6)
5 Rate of increase in speed (12)
6 Imprecise (7)
7 Ebullience (13)
8 Squint harder (anag) (12)
14 Remove a difficulty (7)
16 Happen again (6)
18 A satellite of Uranus (5)

No. 59

Across

1 Linear measures of three feet (5)
4 Decided based on little evidence (7)
7 Devoutly religious (5)
8 Reduce massively in numbers (8)
9 Religious doctrine (5)
11 Deep ditches (8)
15 Portable device to keep the rain off (8)
17 Apprehended with certainty (5)
19 Most precipitous (8)
20 Chris ___ : DJ and TV presenter (5)
21 Petitions to God (7)
22 Eyelashes (5)

Down

1 Criterion (9)
2 Saves from danger (7)
3 Organ of digestion (7)
4 Mild or kind (6)
5 Aromatic flavourings (6)
6 Escape from (5)
10 Large hairy spider (9)
12 Poisonous metallic element (7)
13 Merry (7)
14 A score (6)
16 Devices that cause motion (6)
18 At no time (5)

No. 60

Across

1 Left side of a ship (4)
3 Teaches (8)
9 Permits to travel (7)
10 Titles (5)
11 Pertaining to letters (12)
13 Type of nursery (6)
15 Third sign of the zodiac (6)
17 Question in great detail (5-7)
20 Expressing emotions (of poetry) (5)
21 Large German city (7)
22 Eternal (8)
23 Heavenly body (4)

Down

1 Very small amount of money (8)
2 Repeat something once more (5)
4 Sprints (6)
5 Significant (12)
6 Kettledrums (7)
7 Neither good nor bad (2-2)
8 Highly abstract (12)
12 Appointed member of the House of Lords (4,4)
14 Tympanic membrane (7)
16 Barriers (6)
18 Gold block (5)
19 Move rapidly (4)

CROSSWORD

No. 61

Across

1 Marble (anag) (6)
7 Go past another car (8)
8 Louse egg (3)
9 Songbird with a spotted breast (6)
10 ___ in: confines (4)
11 Brazilian dance (5)
13 Belief (7)
15 Floral (7)
17 Posed a question (5)
21 Roald ___ : author (4)
22 Part of a stamen (6)
23 A knight (3)
24 Tranquillity (8)
25 ___ Moon: Character in Frasier (6)

Down

1 Grates on (6)
2 Opposite of top (6)
3 Scoundrel (5)
4 Fashion anew (7)
5 Engravings (8)
6 With hands on the hips (6)
12 Perplex (8)
14 Printed mistake (7)
16 Old measure of distance (6)
18 Brandy distilled from cherries (6)
19 Magnitude (6)
20 Spirited horse (5)

64

No. 62

Across

1 Not difficult (4)
3 Playhouses (8)
9 Livid (7)
10 Polite and courteous (5)
11 Become ready to eat (of fruit) (5)
12 A curse; wicked look (4,3)
13 Entangle (6)
15 Change rapidly from one position to another (6)
17 West Indian musical style (7)
18 Put in considerable effort (5)
20 Requirements (5)
21 Stations where journeys end (7)
22 Quotidian (8)
23 Highly excited (4)

Down

1 Fizz (13)
2 Dispose of (5)
4 Youth ___ : accommodation provider (6)
5 Practice of designing buildings (12)
6 Critiques (7)
7 25th anniversary of marriage (6,7)
8 Baked product containing seasoned meat (7,5)
14 ___ Klass: TV presenter (7)
16 ___ mundum: defying everyone (6)
19 Cake decoration (5)

No. 63

Across

1 Burnish (6)
7 Completely preoccupied with (8)
8 Grassland (3)
9 Take small bites out of (6)
10 Suggestive (4)
11 Took illegally (5)
13 Coolness (7)
15 Implement (7)
17 Lived (anag) (5)
21 Mythical creature (4)
22 Legendary king of Britain (6)
23 Hair style (3)
24 Green vegetable (8)
25 Apprehend someone (6)

Down

1 People who fly aeroplanes (6)
2 Rough shelter (4-2)
3 Pastime (5)
4 Intrinsic nature (7)
5 Keep at a distance (8)
6 Responds to (6)
12 Clemency (8)
14 Deny any responsibility for (7)
16 Big cats (6)
18 Oral (6)
19 Move slowly and awkwardly (6)
20 Set of moral principles (5)

No. 64

Across

1 Ill manners (11)
9 Gave out playing cards (5)
10 Employ (3)
11 Recurrent topic (5)
12 Garners (5)
13 Extreme audacity (8)
16 Symmetrical open plane curve (8)
18 Enclosed (5)
21 Service colour of the army (5)
22 One and one (3)
23 Porcelain (5)
24 Easily made angry (3-8)

Down

2 Having solidified from lava (of rock) (7)
3 Virtuoso solo passage (7)
4 Country in E Africa (6)
5 Teacher (5)
6 Vapour bath (5)
7 Papal state (7,4)
8 Celebrity (11)
14 Parcel (7)
15 Newsworthy (7)
17 Chamber of the heart (6)
19 Minute pore (5)
20 A gold coin (5)

CROSSWORD

No. 65

Across

1 Low-spirited (8)
5 Move fast in a straight line (4)
9 Symbol (5)
10 Expect; think that (5)
11 Strict isolation (10)
14 Attribute to (6)
15 In a lively manner (6)
17 Kept up (10)
20 Foreign language (slang) (5)
21 Mark ___ : Samuel Langhorne Clemens (5)
22 Egg centre (4)
23 Inaccurately (8)

Down

1 Government tax (4)
2 Jest (4)
3 Act of discussing something; deliberation (12)
4 Mistakes (6)
6 Crucial (8)
7 Intensified (8)
8 Occurring at the same time (12)
12 Gloomily (8)
13 Not obligatory (8)
16 Capital of Austria (6)
18 Indian garment (4)
19 Solely (4)

No. 66

Across

1 Italian acknowledgement (4)
3 Piece of jewellery (8)
9 Tragedy by Shakespeare (7)
10 ___ Robson: British tennis player (5)
11 Accumulate (5)
12 Incrementing; elevating (7)
13 Reply (6)
15 Red dog (anag) (6)
17 Puts money into a venture (7)
18 Seashore (5)
20 Strange and mysterious (5)
21 Explain in detail (7)
22 Christmas season (8)
23 Remain in the same place (4)

Down

1 Relatively (13)
2 Capital of Ghana (5)
4 Urge (6)
5 Children's toy (12)
6 Funny (7)
7 In an inflated manner (13)
8 Re-evaluation (12)
14 More than two (7)
16 Climb (6)
19 Mature human (5)

CROSSWORD

No. 67

Across

1 Suppurate (6)
7 Unproven (8)
8 Female kangaroo (3)
9 Arranged like rays (6)
10 Gelatinous substance (4)
11 Hawaiian greeting (5)
13 Hopes to achieve (7)
15 Serving no purpose (7)
17 Add coal to a fire (5)
21 Clothing (4)
22 Turn down (6)
23 Pub (3)
24 Expression of gratitude (5,3)
25 Book of accounts (6)

Down

1 Soft felt hat (6)
2 Dual audio (6)
3 Angry dispute (3-2)
4 Designer of trendy clothes (7)
5 Author (8)
6 Recreate (6)
12 Recklessly determined (4-4)
14 Fish-eating birds of prey (7)
16 Attack with severe criticism (6)
18 In the ___ : about to happen (6)
19 Breadwinner (6)
20 Paula ___ : US singer (5)

No. 68

Across

1 Cheapest berth on a ship (8)
5 Uproarious party (4)
8 The ___ Roundabout: children's TV show (5)
9 Human-like robot (7)
10 Gap in rocks (7)
12 Lever operated with the foot (7)
14 Boxing up (7)
16 Strut about (7)
18 Figurative language (7)
19 Remains of an old building (5)
20 Metal fastener (4)
21 Preliminary speech (8)

Down

1 Unspecified in number (4)
2 Machine that produces motion (6)
3 Taping (9)
4 Quick look (6)
6 Infinitesimally small (6)
7 Mammal with a spiny coat (8)
11 Let oracle (anag) (9)
12 Actor (8)
13 Type of sausage (6)
14 Religious act of petition (6)
15 Doing nothing (6)
17 Arthur ___ : former US tennis player (4)

CROSSWORD

No. 69

Across

1 Slippery fish (pl) (4)
3 Marriage ceremony (8)
9 Takes away (7)
10 School tests (5)
11 Comprehensible (12)
13 Military greeting (6)
15 Amended (6)
17 Heartbroken (12)
20 Country whose capital is Tripoli (5)
21 Overturned (7)
22 Recently married (5-3)
23 Microscopic organism (4)

Down

1 Soonest (8)
2 Threshold (5)
4 Small finch (6)
5 Ate excessively (12)
6 Promising actress (7)
7 Be at a ___ : be puzzled (4)
8 Developmental (12)
12 Additional book matter (8)
14 Archer's weapon (7)
16 Guarantee (6)
18 Move out of the way (5)
19 Close-knit group of families (4)

No. 70

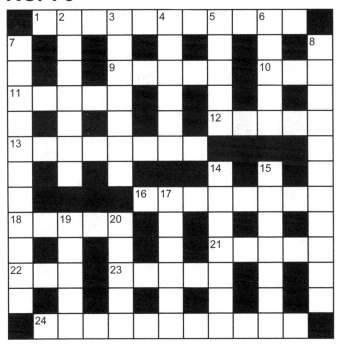

Across

1 Formal declaration (11)
9 Musical note (5)
10 Use a chair (3)
11 Additional (5)
12 Levy (5)
13 Messy and untidy (of appearance) (8)
16 US state (8)
18 Abatement (5)
21 ___ Klum: supermodel (5)
22 Bath vessel (3)
23 Seemingly (combining form) (5)
24 Uninvited guest (11)

Down

2 Chain of flowers (7)
3 People in jail (7)
4 Pertaining to the mind (6)
5 Entice to do something (5)
6 Start of (5)
7 Coarse cotton gauze (11)
8 Testimony (11)
14 Mischievous children (7)
15 Bone in the ear (7)
17 Cream pastry (6)
19 Leg bone (5)
20 Wound the pride of (5)

CROSSWORD

No. 71

Across

1 ___ with: supported (5)
4 Flavouring from a crocus (7)
7 Smart; hurt (5)
8 Person honoured for an achievement (8)
9 Unit of length (5)
11 Church musician (8)
15 Very large (8)
17 Iffy (5)
19 Apportioned (8)
20 Very holy person (5)
21 Wood cutters (7)
22 The Norwegian language (5)

Down

1 Believed (a lie) (9)
2 Share information (7)
3 Land retained by a lord (7)
4 Strikes firmly (6)
5 Male parent (6)
6 Possessor (5)
10 Explain clearly (9)
12 Animal fat (7)
13 Stammer (7)
14 Business organisation (6)
16 Ice homes (6)
18 Barack ___ : 44th US President (5)

No. 72

Across

1 Rubbish containers (4)
3 Adult male horse (8)
9 Isolate (7)
10 Data entered into a system (5)
11 Science of biological processes (12)
13 Respectable; satisfactory (6)
15 Deciduous flowering shrub (6)
17 Lawfully (12)
20 Weatherproof coat (5)
21 Guglielmo ___ : radio pioneer (7)
22 Abruptly (8)
23 Document of ownership (4)

Down

1 Meddlesome person (8)
2 Tortilla topped with cheese (5)
4 ___ Barlow: English actress (6)
5 Governmental abstention from interfering in the free market (7-5)
6 Endanger (7)
7 Eg pecan and cashew (4)
8 Establish as genuine (12)
12 Spotted beetle (8)
14 Removed an obstruction (7)
16 Dreary (6)
18 Call forth or cause (5)
19 Primates (4)

75

No. 73

Across

1 Simpleton (4)
3 Distinction; high status (8)
9 Manned (7)
10 Country in the Himalayas (5)
11 Pure love (5)
12 Recording on tape (7)
13 Deviate suddenly (6)
15 Good luck charm (6)
17 Adventurous journey (7)
18 Garment worn in the kitchen (5)
20 Burning (5)
21 Emotional stability (7)
22 Hostilities (8)
23 Natter (4)

Down

1 Unemotional (13)
2 Camel-like animal (5)
4 Change (6)
5 Not catching fire easily (3-9)
6 Pertaining to marriage (7)
7 The ___ : intellectual movement (13)
8 Bubbling (12)
14 Paradise in Greek mythology (7)
16 Farewell remark (3-3)
19 Cattle-breeding farm (5)

No. 74

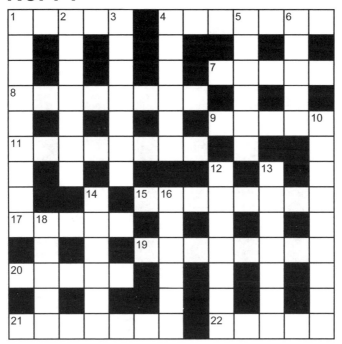

Across

1 Collection of songs (5)
4 Procedure; standard (7)
7 Chuck (5)
8 Exclamations of protest (8)
9 Removes moisture (5)
11 Slender coiling leaves (8)
15 Timetable (8)
17 Grind the teeth together (5)
19 Desert in southern Africa (8)
20 Tablets (5)
21 Pipe from which water can be drawn (7)
22 Flat circular plates (5)

Down

1 Apportioning (9)
2 Rowing or sailing for pleasure (7)
3 Reflects (7)
4 Revoke (6)
5 Lightweight garment (1-5)
6 Loop with a running knot (5)
10 Secondary occupations (9)
12 Introduced air to (7)
13 Clergymen (7)
14 Stableman (6)
16 Wooden house (6)
18 Clamorous (5)

No. 75

Across

1 Country whose capital is Havana (4)
3 Large game bird (8)
9 Destructive (7)
10 Lively Bohemian dance (5)
11 Strong desires (5)
12 Pencil rubbers (7)
13 Uncultivated (of land) (6)
15 Murmur (6)
17 Decide firmly (7)
18 Jessica ___-Hill : British heptathlete (5)
20 African country whose capital is Niamey (5)
21 Italian red wine (7)
22 Prayer service (8)
23 ___ Seacrest: host of American Idol (4)

Down

1 Line that bounds a circle (13)
2 Existing (5)
4 Makes a sibilant sound (6)
5 Using both letters and numerals (12)
6 Illness (7)
7 Violation of a law (13)
8 Upper chamber in Parliament (5,2,5)
14 Layered pasta dish (7)
16 Ordained minister (6)
19 Nursemaid (5)

No. 76

CROSSWORD

Across

1 Inopportune (8)
5 Long narrative poem (4)
8 Female relatives (5)
9 Render perplexed (7)
10 Cost (7)
12 Unrecoverable money owed (3,4)
14 Chilled desserts (7)
16 Deadlock (7)
18 Breathed in (7)
19 Foolishly credulous (5)
20 Adult male singing voice (4)
21 Device recording distance travelled (8)

Down

1 US state (4)
2 Intend (anag) (6)
3 Fails to look after properly (9)
4 Finch (6)
6 Country where one finds Warsaw (6)
7 Tanks for storing water (8)
11 Pen name (9)
12 Roman building (8)
13 Outcome (6)
14 Fixed (6)
15 Severe; stern (6)
17 Beloved; expensive (4)

CROSSWORD

No. 77

Across

1 Go away from quickly (5)
4 Year in which wine was produced (7)
7 Oppress grievously (5)
8 Busiest time on the roads (4,4)
9 Surprising development in a story (5)
11 Disloyal people (8)
15 Unyielding (8)
17 Lines (anag) (5)
19 Heated exchange of views (8)
20 Cat sounds (5)
21 Imposing a tax (7)
22 Brings up (5)

Down

1 Pertaining to the soul (9)
2 Eg from Moscow (7)
3 Broad knife (7)
4 Person who prices things (6)
5 Confused or disconcerted (6)
6 Eg oxygen and nitrogen (5)
10 Menaces (9)
12 ___ bells: orchestral instrument (7)
13 Kneecap (7)
14 Force; vigour (6)
16 Dull and dreary (6)
18 Accustom to something (5)

No. 78

Across

1 Bad habit (4)
3 Potent (8)
9 Coiffure (7)
10 Consent to (5)
11 Heart specialist (12)
14 Cease (3)
16 Type of stopwatch (5)
17 ___ de Cologne: perfume (3)
18 Unnecessarily careful (12)
21 Military trainee (5)
22 Poked (7)
23 Abiding; lasting (8)
24 Parched (4)

Down

1 Eg cars and vans (8)
2 Town ___ : official who makes public announcements (5)
4 Opposite of in (3)
5 Overstatement (12)
6 Envisage (7)
7 Welsh emblem (4)
8 Author of screenplays (12)
12 Assumed proposition (5)
13 Became less intense (8)
15 Separated (7)
19 Command (5)
20 Spots (4)
22 Writing instrument (3)

81

CROSSWORD

No. 79

Across

1 Remedy (4)
3 Shields from (8)
9 Countries (7)
10 Senseless (5)
11 ___ Schmidt: film starring Jack Nicholson (5)
12 Recording (7)
13 Impose or require (6)
15 Religious minister (6)
17 Abundant (7)
18 Remote in manner (5)
20 Metal spikes (5)
21 Large retail stores (7)
22 All people (8)
23 Second-hand (4)

Down

1 Gradual healing (13)
2 Quantitative relation between two amounts (5)
4 Steal livestock (6)
5 Reckless; ready to react violently (7-5)
6 Cup (7)
7 Legerdemain (7,2,4)
8 Luckily (12)
14 Cut of beef (7)
16 Towards the rear (6)
19 Mythical unpleasant giants (5)

No. 80

Across

1	Manages (5)
4	Firmly establish (7)
7	Rinse out (5)
8	Pleasingly rich (8)
9	Carts without sides (5)
11	Moderating; capping (8)
15	Having no worries (8)
17	Andrew Lloyd Webber musical (5)
19	Form of government (8)
20	Completely correct (5)
21	Stupid (7)
22	Extreme fear (5)

Down

1	Polysaccharide forming plant cell walls (9)
2	Suppose to be true (7)
3	Film or play texts (7)
4	Call into question (6)
5	Rephrase (6)
6	Printed insert supplied with a CD (5)
10	Extended one's body (9)
12	Decreased (7)
13	Eg a bishop (7)
14	Plaster for coating walls (6)
16	Pertaining to vinegar (6)
18	Irritated; annoyed (5)

CROSSWORD

No. 81

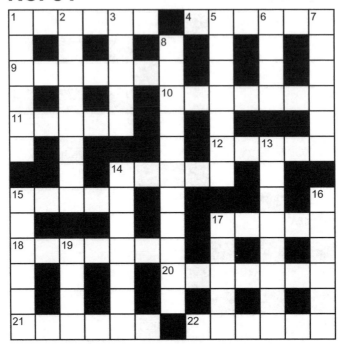

Across

1 Absolve (6)
4 Erase a mark from a surface (6)
9 Corrupt (7)
10 Funnel-shaped river mouth (7)
11 Medicinal ointment (5)
12 Awaken; make excited (5)
14 Breathe heavily at night (5)
15 Frenzied (5)
17 Eg molar or incisor (5)
18 Redecorate (7)
20 Highest mountain (7)
21 Lethargic; sleepy (6)
22 Distilled spirit (6)

Down

1 First born (6)
2 Give courage (8)
3 Long cloud of smoke (5)
5 Fitting (7)
6 Song for a solo voice (4)
7 Biochemical catalyst (6)
8 Item that measures temperature (11)
13 Exposes (8)
14 People who copy out documents (7)
15 Indefinitely large number (6)
16 Talkative (6)
17 Eg incisors and molars (5)
19 Monetary unit of Mexico (4)

No. 82

Across

1 Look at amorously (4)
3 Flag position to indicate mourning (4-4)
9 Make amends (7)
10 Labour organisation (5)
11 Bring together into a mass (12)
14 Mother (3)
16 Residents of an abbey (5)
17 ___ de Janeiro: Brazilian city (3)
18 Indifferent to (12)
21 Stood up (5)
22 Uncertain (7)
23 Official in football (8)
24 Hunted animal (4)

Down

1 Defeat (8)
2 Attractive flower (5)
4 High value playing card (3)
5 Fence closure (anag) (12)
6 Pilot (7)
7 Temporary outside shelter (4)
8 Accepted behaviour whilst dining (5,7)
12 ___ Carlo: area of Monaco (5)
13 Thick cotton fabric (8)
15 Seasonal prevailing wind (7)
19 Belonging to them (5)
20 Opposite of pass (4)
22 North American nation (abbrev) (3)

No. 83

Across

1 Refer to indirectly (6)
4 Cinema guides (6)
9 Dinner party; feast (7)
10 Flatter (7)
11 Valleys (5)
12 Ceases (5)
14 ___ Andronicus: Shakespeare play (5)
15 Welsh breed of dog (5)
17 Emerge from an egg (5)
18 Impeded (7)
20 Guarantees (7)
21 Shove (6)
22 Rode a bike (6)

Down

1 Measure of how strongly an object reflects light (6)
2 More solitary (8)
3 Percussion instruments (5)
5 Eg Poirot and Sherlock Holmes (7)
6 ___ Fitzgerald: famous jazz singer (4)
7 Alarms (6)
8 Having celebrities in attendance (4-7)
13 On the shore of a sea (8)
14 Works in an amateurish way (7)
15 Eg Picasso or Braque (6)
16 Done in stages (6)
17 Hoarse (5)
19 ___ Sharif: Egyptian actor (4)

No. 84

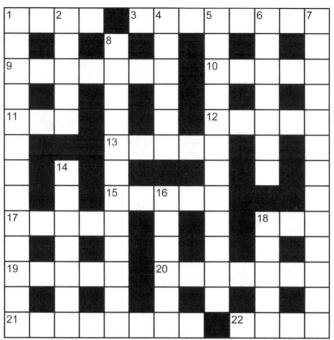

Across

1 Clever remark (4)
3 Reprimanding (8)
9 Levels a charge against (7)
10 Fish basket (5)
11 Beam of light (3)
12 Join together; merge (5)
13 Select; formally approve (5)
15 Fun activities (5)
17 Steer (anag) (5)
18 Small amount of something (3)
19 Path or road (5)
20 Insignificant (7)
21 Large edible marine crustaceans (8)
22 Fit of shivering (4)

Down

1 Four-sided figure (13)
2 Needing to be scratched (5)
4 Gambling house (6)
5 As quickly as possible (7-5)
6 List one by one (7)
7 50th anniversary of a major event (6,7)
8 Separation; alienation (12)
14 Agitate (7)
16 Experienced adviser (6)
18 Undertaking something (5)

No. 85

Across

1 Migratory grasshopper (6)
4 Support (6)
9 Appease (7)
10 Made a guttural sound (7)
11 Loose fibre used in caulking wooden ships (5)
12 Allow entry to (5)
14 Scale representation (5)
15 School of thought (5)
17 Person who goes on long walks (5)
18 Italian fast racing car (7)
20 Rowers (7)
21 Chaos (6)
22 Capital of New South Wales (6)

Down

1 Subatomic particle (6)
2 Excellent (8)
3 Involuntary muscle contraction (5)
5 Act of reading carefully (7)
6 Release; give out (4)
7 Expert in a particular subject (6)
8 Ignored data (anag) (11)
13 Sharpshooter (8)
14 Medium-sized monkey (7)
15 Distort the shape of (6)
16 A parent's Mum (6)
17 Younger son of Prince Charles (5)
19 Optimistic; pink (4)

No. 86

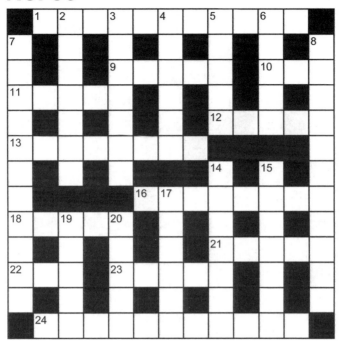

Across

1 Fragility (11)
9 English racetrack (5)
10 Animal foot (3)
11 Denise van ___ : English actress (5)
12 Microscopic fungus (5)
13 Person you work for (8)
16 Large aeroplane (8)
18 Kingdom (5)
21 Hot fluid rock (5)
22 21st Greek letter (3)
23 Cry of excitement (5)
24 Argumentative (11)

Down

2 Excessive bureaucracy (3,4)
3 Crossbar set above a window (7)
4 Find (6)
5 Crazy (5)
6 Reddish-brown colour (5)
7 Compose a dance routine (11)
8 European country (11)
14 Mountain in N Greece (7)
15 Rearranged letters of a word (7)
17 Call on (6)
19 Word of farewell (5)
20 Garden tool (5)

CROSSWORD

No. 87

Across

1 Help or support (6)
7 Demote (8)
8 Deviate off course (3)
9 Greek goddess of wisdom (6)
10 Unit of length (4)
11 Devout (5)
13 Most slothful (7)
15 Servile (7)
17 Foot joint (5)
21 Church recess (4)
22 Agreement or concord (6)
23 Plant liquid (3)
24 Large terrier (8)
25 Spiny-finned fish (6)

Down

1 Purchasing (6)
2 One who is easily frightened (6)
3 Snoops (5)
4 Handbook published annually (7)
5 Action of setting something on fire (8)
6 Adheres to; fastens (6)
12 Stayed longer than necessary (8)
14 Having sharp corners (7)
16 Domestic assistant (2,4)
18 US state with capital Topeka (6)
19 Pass (of time) (6)
20 Strong fibrous tissue (5)

No. 88

Across

1 Exemption (8)
5 Couple (4)
8 ___ Presley: US singer (5)
9 Opening the mouth wide when tired (7)
10 Less quiet (7)
12 Lost (7)
14 Reached a destination (7)
16 Begged (7)
18 Writing fluid holder (7)
19 Remove from school (5)
20 Clean up (4)
21 Recondite (8)

Down

1 Freezes over (4)
2 Films (6)
3 Deteriorated rapidly (9)
4 Attempting (6)
6 Sour to the taste (6)
7 Took into account (8)
11 Rash (9)
12 Centre (8)
13 Culminated (6)
14 Grown-ups (6)
15 Evening star (6)
17 ___ Stewart: ex-England cricketer (4)

CROSSWORD

No. 89

Across

1 Select; choose (4)
3 Arrange by category (8)
9 Approve or support (7)
10 Harsh and grating in sound (5)
11 Overwhelmingly compelling (12)
14 Steal (3)
16 Mixture that insulates soil (5)
17 Nothing (3)
18 Underground (12)
21 Very masculine (5)
22 Chatter (7)
23 Beat out grain (8)
24 Extras (cricket) (4)

Down

1 First public performance (8)
2 ___ of Lebanon: tree (5)
4 Strong alkaline solution (3)
5 Immediately (12)
6 Pancreatic hormone (7)
7 Spool-like toy (2-2)
8 Excessively forward (12)
12 Pertaining to the sun (5)
13 Bed covers (8)
15 Doorman at a nightclub (7)
19 Act of going in (5)
20 Flake of soot (4)
22 ___ chart: type of graph (3)

No. 90

Across

1 Go up in ___ : be destroyed by fire (6)
4 Not rough (6)
9 Term of endearment (informal) (7)
10 Display unit; supervise (7)
11 Remnant of a dying fire (5)
12 Freshwater food fish (5)
14 Religious book (5)
15 Pastoral poem (5)
17 Trite (anag) (5)
18 Art of paper-folding (7)
20 Snuggles (7)
21 Ottawa is the capital here (6)
22 Bushy plant of the mint family (6)

Down

1 Quicker (6)
2 Bitterness of manner (8)
3 Consumer of food (5)
5 Wealthy businessperson (7)
6 Kiln (4)
7 Floor of a fireplace (6)
8 Recalling (11)
13 A cephalopod (8)
14 Cried plaintively (7)
15 Symbolic (6)
16 Botch (4-2)
17 Petulant (5)
19 ___ Lendl: former tennis star (4)

No. 91

1		2				3	4		5		6		7

(grid)

Across

1 A flat float (4)
3 Person who has religious faith (8)
9 Reticular (7)
10 Young male horses (5)
11 Clothing such as a vest (12)
14 Long-leaved lettuce (3)
16 Group of lions (5)
17 Make a mistake (3)
18 Quarrelsome and uncooperative (12)
21 Promotional wording (5)
22 Intoxicating element in wine (7)
23 Absurd representation of something (8)
24 Time periods (4)

Down

1 Repudiate (8)
2 Destined (5)
4 Organ of sight (3)
5 Ineptness (12)
6 Hanging drapery (7)
7 Reckless; skin eruption (4)
8 Discreditable (12)
12 Extraterrestrial (5)
13 Stiff coarse hairs (8)
15 Kitchen implement (7)
19 Opposite one of two (5)
20 Tuba (anag) (4)
22 Small social insect (3)

No. 92

Across

1	Small island (5)
4	Ingenuous (7)
7	Prophet (5)
8	Walked unsteadily (8)
9	Vault under a church (5)
11	Medicine (8)
15	Ocean (8)
17	Announcement (5)
19	Showed a TV show (8)
20	Feign (3,2)
21	Delightful (7)
22	Mortise partner (5)

Down

1	Establish (9)
2	Plundering (7)
3	Statements of intent to harm (7)
4	Seem (6)
5	French museum (6)
6	Remnant of a fallen tree (5)
10	Score in American football (9)
12	King Arthur's home (7)
13	Substitute (5-2)
14	Place of education (6)
16	Plan (6)
18	Celtic priest (5)

No. 93

Across

1 Seethe (4)
3 Casual and relaxed (8)
9 Small fast ship (7)
10 At that place; not here (5)
11 Restore to good condition (12)
13 Bit sharply (6)
15 Recover; get back (6)
17 Junction (12)
20 What Harry Potter might cast (5)
21 Give too much money (7)
22 Answered sharply (8)
23 Lump of earth (4)

Down

1 Statuette (8)
2 Eat steadily (5)
4 Stinging weed (6)
5 Fully extended (12)
6 A very skilled performer (7)
7 Falsehoods (4)
8 Deceiver (6-6)
12 Fully aware (4-4)
14 Acrid (7)
16 On land (6)
18 Drive forward (5)
19 Russian monarch (4)

No. 94

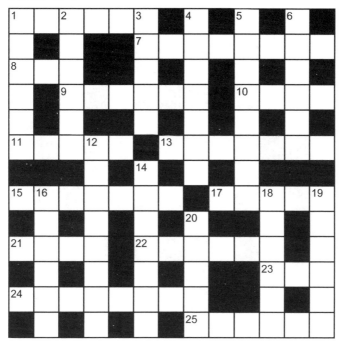

Across

1	Conveying by gestures (6)
7	Inanimate (8)
8	Relieve or free from (3)
9	Functional (6)
10	Fraud (4)
11	Woolly ruminant animal (5)
13	Is present at (7)
15	___ one's nest: enrich oneself (7)
17	Trees (anag); organic compound (5)
21	Fibber (4)
22	Give a new and improved appearance to (6)
23	Fizzy drink (3)
24	Convenience meal (4,4)
25	Surpass (6)

Down

1	Bog; confused situation (6)
2	Self-contained unit (6)
3	Church farmland (5)
4	Personal belongings (7)
5	Close groups (8)
6	Land surrounded by water (6)
12	The whole of something (8)
14	A very long time ago (4,3)
16	___ Wood: US actor (6)
18	Alcoholic drink (6)
19	Uttered coarsely (6)
20	Avoid (5)

No. 95

Across

1   Implement for styling hair (4)
3   Moved forwards (8)
9   Female spirit (7)
10 Many times (5)
11 Art of planning a dance (12)
14 Hearing organ (3)
16 Burst of light (5)
17 23rd Greek letter (3)
18 List of books referred to (12)
21 Nimble (5)
22 Relating to current affairs (7)
23 Took a firm stand (8)
24 Antelopes (4)

Down

1   Small bays (8)
2   Juicy fruit (5)
4   Expected at a certain time (3)
5   Therapeutic use of plant extracts (12)
6   Draw level (5,2)
7   Natural fertiliser (4)
8   Happiness (12)
12 Fertiliser from seabird droppings (5)
13 Two-wheeled vehicles (8)
15 Dried grapes (7)
19 Brown nut (5)
20 Cab (4)
22 Golf peg (3)

No. 96

Across

1 Risky (6)
4 Church buildings (6)
9 Hurtful (7)
10 Comparison (7)
11 Water lily (5)
12 Recommended strongly (5)
14 Sticky sweet liquid (5)
15 Lifting device (5)
17 Receive a ball in one's hands (5)
18 Heavy cotton cloth (7)
20 Flowers with white petals (7)
21 Work hard; toil (6)
22 Complied with a command (6)

Down

1 Domed roof (6)
2 The flying of aircraft (8)
3 Eateries (5)
5 Disperse (5,2)
6 Currency of Spain and Germany (4)
7 Remained in a certain place (6)
8 Recreational areas (11)
13 Tip (8)
14 Trembling (7)
15 Covered with trees (6)
16 Pursued (6)
17 Ascend (5)
19 Scottish singer-songwriter (4)

No. 97

Across

1 Paternal (8)
5 Strict (4)
8 Monastery church (5)
9 Deliberately impassive (7)
10 Subtleties (7)
12 Distribute illicitly (7)
14 Feeling of great happiness (7)
16 Combined two or more metals (7)
18 Exhausted (4,3)
19 Giggle (5)
20 The Christmas festival (4)
21 Dullness of colour (8)

Down

1 Standard (4)
2 Trinidad and ___ : country (6)
3 History of a word (9)
4 A cargo (6)
6 Effect; force (6)
7 The priesthood (8)
11 Awfully (9)
12 Famous street in Manhattan (8)
13 Consisting of flowers (6)
14 Newspaper boss (6)
15 Request earnestly (6)
17 Mosh (anag) (4)

No. 98

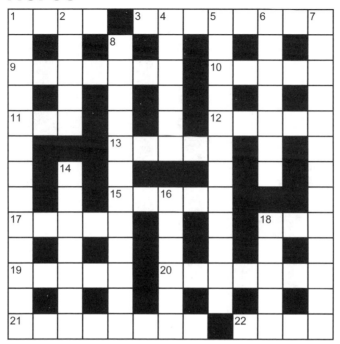

Across

1 Portfolio (4)
3 Inherent (8)
9 Lines of equal pressure on maps (7)
10 Device that splits light (5)
11 Large deer (3)
12 Run away with a lover (5)
13 Our planet (5)
15 Noble gas (5)
17 Praise highly (5)
18 Pronoun used to refer to a ship (3)
19 Indifferent to emotions (5)
20 Young hare (7)
21 Annoying with continual criticism (8)
22 True and actual (4)

Down

1 British comedy author (5,8)
2 Long-legged wading bird (5)
4 Stream (anag) (6)
5 Uneasy (12)
6 Perfect example of a quality (7)
7 Unpredictable (13)
8 Relating to numbers (12)
14 Edible mollusc (7)
16 Unit of volume (6)
18 Powerful forward movement (5)

No. 99

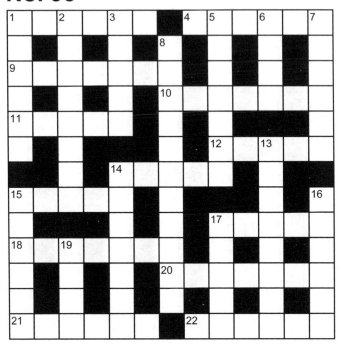

Across

1 Mixes up or confuses (6)
4 Worldwide (6)
9 Resembling dust (7)
10 Receptacle for letters (7)
11 Wading birds (5)
12 Solemn promises (5)
14 Relay device (5)
15 Divide by two (5)
17 Wash one's body in water (5)
18 Foretell (7)
20 Caused to catch fire (7)
21 Sculptured symbols (6)
22 What bees collect (6)

Down

1 Aim to achieve something (6)
2 Sudden heavy rain shower (8)
3 Seven (anag) (5)
5 Secret affair (7)
6 Incandescent lamp (4)
7 Wildcats (6)
8 Compassionate (11)
13 Advocating abstinence from alcohol (8)
14 Cast a spell on (7)
15 Wishing for (6)
16 Deprive of force; stifle (6)
17 Small tuned drum (5)
19 Jealousy (4)

No. 100

Across

1	Bend or coil (4)
3	Cause resentment (8)
9	Ideas (7)
10	Device used to connect to the internet (5)
11	Cairo is in this country (5)
12	Inspire with love (7)
13	Teachers (6)
15	Scuffle (6)
17	Evaded (7)
18	Become less intense (5)
20	Country in southern Asia (5)
21	Books of maps (7)
22	Gibberish (8)
23	Large group or collection (4)

Down

1	Close mental application (13)
2	Hear a court case anew (5)
4	Misdirected (6)
5	Limitless (12)
6	Tiresome (7)
7	Pitilessly (13)
8	Person studying after a first degree (12)
14	Walked upon (7)
16	Standards of perfection (6)
19	Passage between rows of seats (5)

103

No. 101

Across

1 Stride; rate of moving (4)
3 Sit with legs wide apart (8)
9 Capital of Kenya (7)
10 More recent (5)
11 Considerately (12)
13 Sugary flower secretion (6)
15 Rare (6)
17 Demands or needs (12)
20 First Greek letter (5)
21 Evergreen coniferous shrub (7)
22 Worries (8)
23 Coloured (4)

Down

1 Expressing remorse (8)
2 Coarse twilled cotton fabric (5)
4 Pollutes (6)
5 Formal notice (12)
6 Someone who dithers (7)
7 Goes wrong (4)
8 Pay tribute to another (12)
12 Calculated and careful (8)
14 Lower the price of something (7)
16 Inhabitant of Troy (6)
18 Chilly (5)
19 Bathroom mineral powder (4)

No. 102

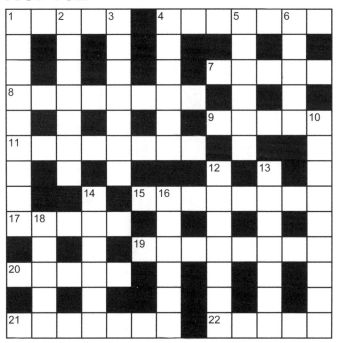

Across

1 Twisted to one side (5)
4 Timidness (7)
7 Flies high (5)
8 Person engaged in a lawsuit (8)
9 Bludgeons (5)
11 Written agreements (8)
15 Criminal (8)
17 Smart and fashionable (informal) (5)
19 Cause frustration (8)
20 Extremely small (prefix) (5)
21 Taking part in a game (7)
22 Stratum (5)

Down

1 Track and field events (9)
2 Needleworker (7)
3 Heavy (7)
4 Absorbent material (6)
5 Pasta strip (6)
6 Cleanse by rubbing (5)
10 Tool used when a pencil is blunt (9)
12 Strongly influencing later developments (7)
13 Perfectly (7)
14 Far from the intended target (6)
16 Sacking (6)
18 Spin around (5)

CROSSWORD

No. 103

Across

1 Redbreasted birds (6)
4 Anew (6)
9 Large household water container (7)
10 Played for time (7)
11 Submerged ridges of rock (5)
12 Disgust (5)
14 Insane (5)
15 Make good on a debt (5)
17 Long tubes (5)
18 Purplish red colour (7)
20 Laughable (7)
21 Number in a football team (6)
22 Evaluate (6)

Down

1 Revived or regenerated (6)
2 Flatter (6,2)
3 Memos (5)
5 Very distant (7)
6 British nobleman (4)
7 George ___ : composer (6)
8 Painting genre (8,3)
13 Tangible (8)
14 Poison (7)
15 Far away (6)
16 Plus points (6)
17 Sends through the mail (5)
19 Adhesive (4)

No. 104

Across

1 Hardens (4)
3 Presiding officer (8)
9 Imaginary creature (7)
10 Ice cream is often served in these (5)
11 Short story or poem for children (7,5)
13 Long strips of cloth (6)
15 Fundamental; essential (6)
17 Emergency touchdown (5-7)
20 Egg-shaped (5)
21 Criminal (7)
22 Re-evaluate (8)
23 Computer memory unit (4)

Down

1 Cosiness (8)
2 One who always puts in a lot of effort (5)
4 History play by Shakespeare (5,1)
5 Incomprehensibly (12)
6 Smallest amount (7)
7 Facial feature (4)
8 Despair (12)
12 Grace (8)
14 Film directed by Stephen Gaghan (7)
16 Hand protectors (6)
18 European country (5)
19 Male hog (4)

CROSSWORD

No. 105

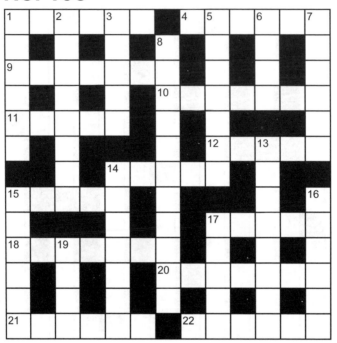

Across

1 Deprive of power (6)
4 Extravagant meals (6)
9 Root vegetable (7)
10 Drop sharply (7)
11 Timber framework (5)
12 ___ Avenue: NY shopping street (5)
14 Midges (5)
15 Love intently (5)
17 Spore-producing organisms (5)
18 Type of natural disaster (7)
20 One's savings for the future (4,3)
21 Observing furtively (6)
22 Seat for two or more persons (6)

Down

1 Repositories (6)
2 Person highly skilled in music (8)
3 Basins (5)
5 Envelops (7)
6 Appear (4)
7 Informer (6)
8 Coming close to (11)
13 Most amusing (8)
14 An edible jelly (7)
15 Lofts (6)
16 Small worry; irritate (6)
17 ___ Way: famous Roman road (5)
19 Unattractive (4)

No. 106

Across

1 Substitute (11)
9 Muscular strength (5)
10 Belonging to us (3)
11 Chop meat into very small pieces (5)
12 Speed (5)
13 Usually (8)
16 Until now (8)
18 Shine brightly (5)
21 Comedian (5)
22 Also (3)
23 Main stem of a tree (5)
24 Eg Huw Edwards and Trevor McDonald (11)

Down

2 Entrap (7)
3 Given generously (7)
4 Place of worship (6)
5 Period of time consisting of 28 - 31 days (5)
6 Sheltered places (5)
7 Basic entitlements for all (5,6)
8 The military (5,6)
14 Amazed (7)
15 Branch of linguistics (7)
17 Resistant to something (6)
19 Decay (5)
20 Apportions a punishment (5)

CROSSWORD

No. 107

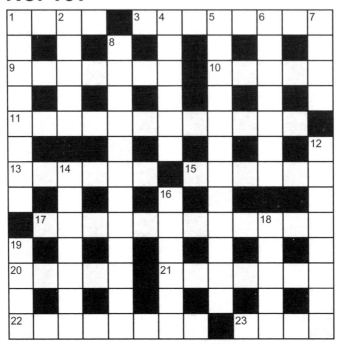

Across

1	Walking stick (4)
3	Gifts (8)
9	Remove garments (7)
10	Humming (5)
11	Someone skilled in penmanship (12)
13	Positive and happy (6)
15	Ought to (6)
17	An idea that is added later (12)
20	Long poems (5)
21	Perennial herb (7)
22	Anxiousness (8)
23	Lyric poems (4)

Down

1	North African semolina (8)
2	Rafael ___ : Spanish tennis star (5)
4	Place that is frequented for holidays (6)
5	Marksman (12)
6	Art ___ : decorative style of art (7)
7	Physical magnitude (4)
8	Food shop (12)
12	Versions of a book (8)
14	Polishing (7)
16	Backless seats (6)
18	Impressive in appearance (5)
19	Give up one's rights (4)

No. 108

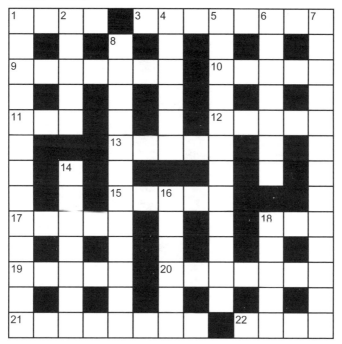

Across

1 Temporary living quarters (4)
3 Synthetic polymeric substances (8)
9 Zeppelin (7)
10 Game of chance (5)
11 Fire residue (3)
12 Fly around a planet (5)
13 Church instrument (5)
15 Ancient object (5)
17 Spanish wine (5)
18 Gone by (of time) (3)
19 Make law (5)
20 Good luck charms (7)
21 Whipped (8)
22 Anxious; nervous (4)

Down

1 Bland and dull (13)
2 Aromatic resin (5)
4 Small pet canine (6)
5 Part of the mind (12)
6 Dishonourable (7)
7 Impulsively (13)
8 Chair proctor (anag) (12)
14 Pear-shaped fruit (7)
16 Place where something is set (6)
18 Alter (5)

CROSSWORD

No. 109

Across

1 Brood (4)
3 Weapon (8)
9 Backtrack (7)
10 Soothes (5)
11 Feeling let down (12)
14 Used to be (3)
16 Number after seven (5)
17 Sense of self-esteem (3)
18 Having an acrid wit (5-7)
21 Yellow citrus fruit (5)
22 Plausible; defensible (7)
23 Dish of rice with fish and eggs (8)
24 Spherical objects (4)

Down

1 A reduction in price (8)
2 Golf shots (5)
4 Rodent (3)
5 Without parallel (6,2,4)
6 Accept to be true (7)
7 Cardinal point (4)
8 Re-emergence (12)
12 Should (5)
13 Lack of warmth (8)
15 Planned one's actions (7)
19 Brown earth pigment (5)
20 Anti-aircraft fire (4)
22 Draw (3)

No. 110

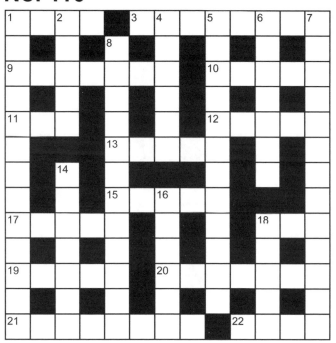

CROSSWORD

Across

1 Become dim (4)
3 Soak; drench (8)
9 Faithfulness (7)
10 Be alive; be real (5)
11 Possess (3)
12 Plants of a region (5)
13 Lumberjack (5)
15 Cavalry sword (5)
17 Freshwater fish (5)
18 Commander; chief (3)
19 Beneath (5)
20 Greatest in height (7)
21 Fence formed by bushes (8)
22 Small whirlpool (4)

Down

1 Continue a stroke in tennis (6,7)
2 Most respected person in a field (5)
4 In a careless manner (6)
5 Intuitively designed (of a system) (4-8)
6 US state (7)
7 Wastefully; lavishly (13)
8 Framework for washed garments (7,5)
14 Stashed away (7)
16 Inexpensive restaurant (6)
18 In front (5)

No. 111

Across

1 Weapons (4)
3 Italian cheese (8)
9 Oceanic birds (7)
10 Loans (anag) (5)
11 ___ John: pop star (5)
12 Graceful in form (7)
13 Person after whom a discovery is named (6)
15 Large property with land (6)
17 Protective CD covers (7)
18 Angered; irritated (5)
20 Sink (5)
21 Unfamiliar (7)
22 Lift (8)
23 ___ Campbell: Scream actress (4)

Down

1 Capable of being understood (13)
2 Short choral composition (5)
4 Jane ___ : English novelist (6)
5 Coup (12)
6 Seedless raisin (7)
7 Failure to be present at (13)
8 US state (12)
14 Supervise (7)
16 Old Portuguese currency (6)
19 Not tense (5)

No. 112

Across

1 Ponder (8)
5 Sound reflection (4)
8 Accurate pieces of information (5)
9 Stuffy (7)
10 Forgives for a fault (7)
12 Friendless (7)
14 Runs out (7)
16 Provoked; encouraged (7)
18 Regimes (anag) (7)
19 Fill with high spirits (5)
20 ___ Berra: baseball player (4)
21 Fits in place (8)

Down

1 Part of a sleeve (4)
2 Five cent coin (US) (6)
3 Bankrupt (9)
4 Deleted (6)
6 Wrinkle in an item of clothing (6)
7 Thinks about something continually (8)
11 Part (9)
12 Foolishly (8)
13 Hurting (6)
14 Thomas ___ : US inventor (6)
15 Sell to the public (6)
17 Disorder; confused situation (4)

No. 113

	1	2		3		4		5		6		
7												8
				9						10		
11												
								12				
13												
								14		15		
					16	17						
18		19		20								
								21				
22				23								
	24											

Across

1 Shipment (11)
9 Wide-awake (5)
10 Hair colourant (3)
11 Alters (5)
12 Type of military operation (5)
13 Parroted (anag) (8)
16 Type of pasta (8)
18 Reclining (5)
21 Latin American dance (5)
22 Distinct historical period (3)
23 Animal life of a region (5)
24 Calm and sensible (5-6)

Down

2 Most favourable (7)
3 Beach area (7)
4 Poor district (6)
5 Tiny arachnids (5)
6 Prod with the elbow (5)
7 Dejected (11)
8 Having definite limits (11)
14 Eyelash cosmetic (7)
15 Decorative framework (7)
17 Surprise attack (6)
19 Visual representation (5)
20 Blunder (5)

No. 114

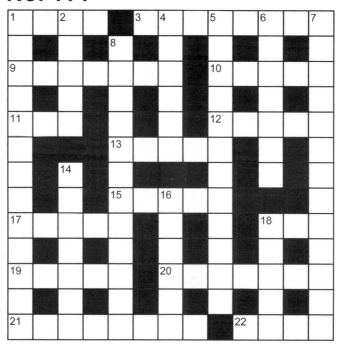

Across

1 Court enclosure (4)
3 Recurring at intervals (8)
9 Tried a new product (7)
10 Big cat (5)
11 Small spot (3)
12 Imitative of the past (5)
13 Unit of heat (5)
15 Large body of water (5)
17 Legal process (5)
18 Signal for action (3)
19 Obtains something desirable (5)
20 Famous Italian astronomer (7)
21 Broke down food (8)
22 Burden (4)

Down

1 Deprived (13)
2 Celestial body (5)
4 Undergo a hardship (6)
5 Unending (12)
6 Not analogue (7)
7 Period of the Paleozoic Era (13)
8 Decomposition by a current (12)
14 Grinning (7)
16 Regime (anag) (6)
18 Large intestine (5)

117

No. 115

Across

1 Word ending a prayer (4)
3 Dress clothes (4,4)
9 Group of three plays (7)
10 Type of plastic; record (5)
11 Beguile (5)
12 Perfect happiness (7)
13 Urges to do something (6)
15 Afternoon sleep (6)
17 Decorative style of the 1920s and 1930s (3,4)
18 Shallow recess (5)
20 Plump (5)
21 Bring up; rear (7)
22 Lenience (8)
23 Tiny social insects (4)

Down

1 Not living up to expectations (13)
2 ___ Dushku: actress (5)
4 Gainly (anag) (6)
5 Designed to distract (12)
6 Plants that live a year or less (7)
7 Conscious knowledge of oneself (4-9)
8 Preservative (12)
14 Drinkable (7)
16 Brandy (6)
19 Stir milk (5)

No. 116

Across

1	Withdraws (8)
5	___ Major: the Great Bear (4)
9	Put an idea in someone's mind (5)
10	Sailing vessel (5)
11	Managed carefully (10)
14	Three-legged support for a camera (6)
15	Imminent danger (6)
17	Fervent (10)
20	Dried kernel of the coconut (5)
21	Hold on to tightly (5)
22	In ___ : instead (4)
23	Wheeled supermarket vehicles (8)

Down

1	Engrossed (4)
2	Confine; snare (4)
3	Relating to horoscopes (12)
4	Attributes (6)
6	Recollected (8)
7	Remedy to a poison (8)
8	Conjectural (12)
12	Not usual (8)
13	___ Verdi: composer (8)
16	Situated within a building (6)
18	Frost (4)
19	Hens lay these (4)

119

No. 117

Across

1 Every (4)
3 Clover-like plant (8)
9 Vacuum flask (7)
10 Exit (5)
11 Despicable (12)
14 Of recent origin (3)
16 Reel for winding yarn (5)
17 Our star (3)
18 Importance (12)
21 Prevent (5)
22 Indigenous people (7)
23 Intelligentsia (8)
24 Unfortunately (4)

Down

1 Tempting (8)
2 Remove dirt (5)
4 Belonging to him (3)
5 A large number (12)
6 Prophets (7)
7 Flat-bottomed boat (4)
8 Imitator (12)
12 Factual evidence (5)
13 Opposites (8)
15 Palest (7)
19 A central point (5)
20 ___ Scholes: former England footballer (4)
22 Ten (anag) (3)

No. 118

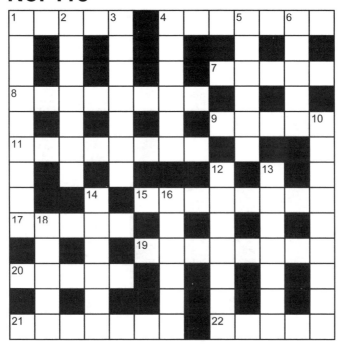

CROSSWORD

Across

1	Cooked in the oven (5)
4	Humorous; done in fun (7)
7	Bands worn around the waist (5)
8	Beneficiaries of a will (8)
9	___ Allan Poe: US writer (5)
11	Views about something (8)
15	Feud (8)
17	Floating timber platforms (5)
19	Respected and admired (8)
20	Agreeable sound or tune (5)
21	Revitalised (7)
22	Bandage for an injured arm (5)

Down

1	Earthmover (9)
2	Central bolt (7)
3	Refuse container (7)
4	Clay ___ : shooting target (6)
5	Gives in (6)
6	Favouring extreme views (5)
10	Gratifying (9)
12	Commercials (7)
13	Nerve impulses (7)
14	Band of colour (6)
16	Followed (6)
18	Severe (5)

CROSSWORD

No. 119

Across

1 Overly concerned with detail (8)
5 Cooking pots (4)
8 Group of eight (5)
9 Bridgelike structure (7)
10 ___ May: Prime Minister (7)
12 Eg Paula Radcliffe (7)
14 Shorten (7)
16 Reduced in value (7)
18 Assembly of people (7)
19 Epic poem ascribed to Homer (5)
20 Price (4)
21 Small flesh-eating mammal (8)

Down

1 Walk with heavy steps (4)
2 Disengage (6)
3 Substances that promote growth (9)
4 Ask a person to come (6)
6 Entertains (6)
7 Capable of being satisfied (8)
11 Etching into a material (9)
12 Pertaining to education (8)
13 Superior of a nunnery (6)
14 In slow time (of music) (6)
15 Gaming tile (6)
17 Lazy (4)

No. 120

Across

1 A magical quality (8)
5 Study assiduously (4)
9 Blood vessels (5)
10 Employer (5)
11 Transformation (10)
14 Series of subject lessons (6)
15 Frightened (6)
17 Moving staircases (10)
20 Browned bread (5)
21 High lending practice (5)
22 Snooker players use these (4)
23 Cold-blooded animals (8)

Down

1 Salvage (4)
2 Alliance between nations (4)
3 Very sad (12)
4 Abandon a plan (6)
6 Fighters (8)
7 A lament (8)
8 Malfunction or fail (of an electrical device) (5-7)
12 Choosing from various sources (8)
13 Buy (8)
16 Walk with long steps (6)
18 Select from a large amount (4)
19 Hair colourants (4)

CROSSWORD

No. 121

Across

1	Respectful (11)
9	Move on hands and knees (5)
10	Show discontent (3)
11	Mexican plant fibre (5)
12	Give a solemn oath (5)
13	Cutting instrument (8)
16	Assign (8)
18	The prevailing fashion (5)
21	Instruct (5)
22	High ball in tennis (3)
23	Speak (5)
24	Perceptive; insightful (11)

Down

2	Flexible (7)
3	Shut in (7)
4	Pencil rubber (6)
5	Informs (5)
6	Stroll (5)
7	Compulsively (11)
8	Camaraderie (11)
14	Ballroom dance (7)
15	Marmoset (7)
17	Linger aimlessly (6)
19	Triangular wall part (5)
20	Display freely (5)

No. 122

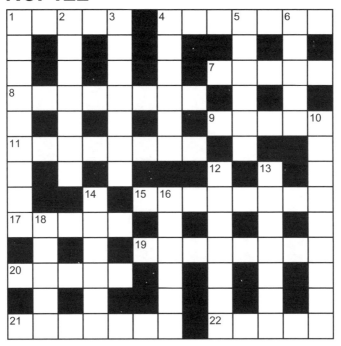

Across

1 Anxious (5)
4 Deliberately cruel (7)
7 Isle of ___ : island near Southampton (5)
8 Skin care product (8)
9 Smug smile (5)
11 Similarity between different things (8)
15 Lumberjack's tool (8)
17 Item of clothing (5)
19 Spread out (8)
20 Besmirch (5)
21 Learner (7)
22 Large waterbirds (5)

Down

1 Bulbous plant (9)
2 Restores honour (7)
3 Not as old (7)
4 Coating (6)
5 Expressions (6)
6 Law court official (5)
10 General erudition (9)
12 Biting sharply (7)
13 Assign (7)
14 Short trip to perform a task (6)
16 Altitude (6)
18 Tidily kept (5)

CROSSWORD

125

CROSSWORD

No. 123

Across

1 Electrically charged particles (4)
3 SE Asian country (8)
9 Dissolution of a marriage (7)
10 Solid blow (5)
11 Seals (anag) (5)
12 Be subjected to (7)
13 Made good on a debt (6)
15 Engineless aircraft (6)
17 Took along (7)
18 Empty spaces (5)
20 Shout of appreciation (5)
21 Greed (7)
22 Longing (8)
23 Doubtful (4)

Down

1 Inexpressibly (13)
2 Original; new (5)
4 Street (6)
5 Ancient and old-fashioned (12)
6 Stimulated; urged on (7)
7 In a suitable manner (13)
8 Scolding (8-4)
14 Proportionately (3,4)
16 Make an unusually great effort (6)
19 Leader or ruler (5)

No. 124

Across

1	Heavy (6)
4	Wall painting or mural (6)
9	Playful musical compositions (7)
10	Shine faintly (7)
11	Dismiss from office (5)
12	Walks awkwardly (5)
14	Firearm (5)
15	Topic (5)
17	Remove wool from sheep (5)
18	Most profound (7)
20	Understanding of another (7)
21	Strangest (6)
22	Calm (6)

Down

1	Person to whom a lease is granted (6)
2	They compete in the Olympic Games (8)
3	White waterbird (5)
5	Embryonic root (7)
6	Slender (4)
7	Musical dramas (6)
8	Nimble; fast (5-6)
13	Imposing (8)
14	Retreats (7)
15	Dark blue dye (6)
16	Made a request to God (6)
17	Flower part; pales (anag) (5)
19	___ Blyton: writer (4)

No. 125

Across

1 Starve (6)
7 Whole numbers (8)
8 Creature with pointed ears (3)
9 Chap (6)
10 Religious sisters (4)
11 Pick out; choose (5)
13 Cargo (7)
15 Earthly (7)
17 County in E England (5)
21 South American country (4)
22 Confer holy orders on (6)
23 Mammal with a bushy tail (3)
24 Squid dish (8)
25 Constructs (6)

Down

1 Turn to ice (6)
2 Make a sound quieter (6)
3 Mountainous (5)
4 Person who looks after the passengers on a ship (7)
5 Business organisations (8)
6 Soak (6)
12 Pertaining to the arts (8)
14 Distant runner-up (4-3)
16 Unidirectional (3-3)
18 Wicked (6)
19 Ancient Persian king (6)
20 Speak in public without preparation (2-3)

No. 126

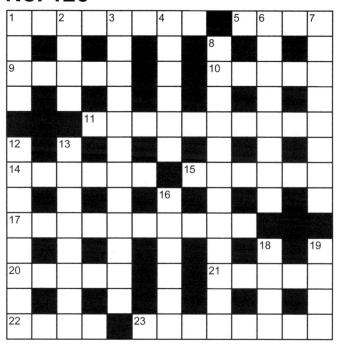

Across

1 An ordinary person (8)
5 A large amount (4)
9 Show triumphant joy (5)
10 The Hunter (constellation) (5)
11 Changeable and unpredictable (10)
14 Refrigerator compartment (6)
15 Beat with the fists (6)
17 Unselfish in manner (10)
20 Vertical part of a step (5)
21 Short musical composition (5)
22 Possesses (4)
23 Plump (4-4)

Down

1 Cook (4)
2 Heavy hammer (4)
3 Outsmart (12)
4 Small shrubs with pithy stems (6)
6 Specified work outfits (8)
7 Truly (8)
8 Decisively (12)
12 Leonardo ___ : actor (8)
13 Discard; abandon (8)
16 Not genuine (6)
18 Greek spirit (4)
19 Depend on (4)

129

CROSSWORD

No. 127

Across

1   ___ stone: means of advancement (8)
5   Matured (4)
8   Underground enlarged stem (5)
9   Explanations (7)
10 Spacecraft that circles the planet (7)
12 In an unspecified manner (7)
14 Hit hard (7)
16 Liked by many people (7)
18 Metal similar to platinum (7)
19 Lazes; does nothing (5)
20 Lesion (4)
21 Dawdlers (8)

Down

1   Locate or place (4)
2   Symbol or representation (6)
3   Narrow-minded (9)
4   Limited in scope (6)
6   Process of increasing in size (6)
7   Disloyal person (8)
11 Sense of ___ : affinity for a particular place (9)
12 Losing grip (8)
13 Breaks apart forcibly (6)
14 Black Sea peninsula (6)
15 Apparatus for heating water (6)
17 Requests (4)

No. 128

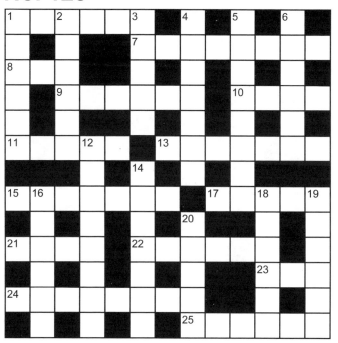

Across

1 Pygmy chimpanzee (6)
7 Terminated (8)
8 ___ Tyler: actress (3)
9 Restaurant (6)
10 Female sheep (pl) (4)
11 Ashley ___ : actress (5)
13 Contemptuously (7)
15 White and lustrous (hair) (7)
17 Widespread dislike (5)
21 Frozen rain (4)
22 Majestic; wonderful (6)
23 Sprite (3)
24 Re-emerge (8)
25 Assent or agree to (6)

Down

1 Lively Spanish dance (6)
2 Books (6)
3 Proposal (5)
4 Desiring what someone else has (7)
5 Climbed (8)
6 Expose (6)
12 Wrapper for a letter (8)
14 Traversed (7)
16 Pictorial representations (6)
18 Drink (6)
19 Long-tailed crow (6)
20 Dramatic musical work (5)

131

CROSSWORD

No. 129

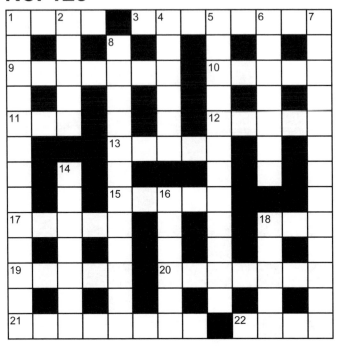

Across

1 Snug (4)
3 Frozen dessert (3,5)
9 Sailor (7)
10 Hushed (5)
11 Impertinence (slang) (3)
12 Inactive (5)
13 Certain to fail (2-3)
15 Small arm of the sea (5)
17 Ben ___ : Scottish mountain (5)
18 ___ Ivanovic: tennis player (3)
19 Sky-blue colour (5)
20 Anthropoid (7)
21 Boating (8)
22 Church song (4)

Down

1 Given free of charge (13)
2 Parts (anag) (5)
4 Wading bird with a long beak (6)
5 Blends; mixtures (12)
6 Very great (7)
7 Largest inland sea (13)
8 Not staying the same throughout (12)
14 Temporary camp (7)
16 Non-ordained Church member (6)
18 Friendship (5)

No. 130

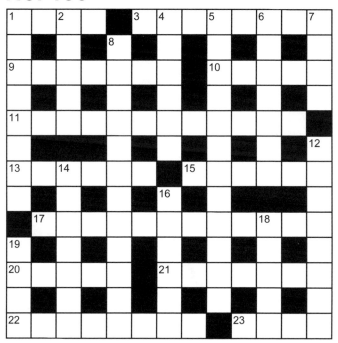

Across

1 Garment for the foot (4)
3 Bridge-like structures (8)
9 Aural pain (7)
10 Ethical (5)
11 Very eager; keen (12)
13 Attack someone (6)
15 Alyssa ___ : Phoebe in Charmed (6)
17 Extension (12)
20 Moth-___ : damaged (5)
21 Wavering effect in a musical tone (7)
22 An indirect and sometimes snide implication (8)
23 Saw; observed (4)

Down

1 Emaciated (8)
2 Mark of insertion (5)
4 Spain and Portugal (6)
5 Tamed (12)
6 Birthplace of Napoleon (7)
7 River sediment (4)
8 Person one knows (12)
12 Retrieve a file from the internet (8)
14 Lessen (7)
16 Joined together (6)
18 Creamy-white colour (5)
19 Round before the final (abbrev) (4)

133

No. 131

Across

1 Brushing the coat of (an animal) (8)
5 Point-winning serves (tennis) (4)
9 Move back and forth (5)
10 More pleasant (5)
11 Military officer (4-2-4)
14 Continue to exist (6)
15 Caress (6)
17 Curved pieces of wood (10)
20 Simple (5)
21 Speed music is played at (5)
22 Jedi Master in Star Wars films (4)
23 Money in use in a country (8)

Down

1 Core meaning (4)
2 Leave out (4)
3 Grandeur (12)
4 Tensed (anag) (6)
6 White crested parrot (8)
7 ___ for cash: short of money (8)
8 Detective (12)
12 Very likely (8)
13 Decorated with a raised design (8)
16 Capital of the Bahamas (6)
18 Portent (4)
19 Prying; overly curious (4)

No. 132

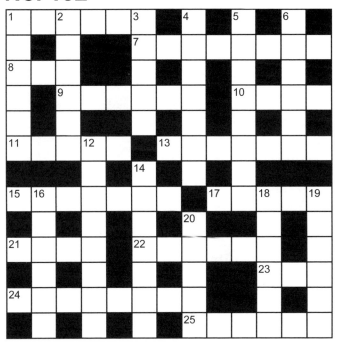

Across

1 Hot pepper (6)
7 Astronaut (8)
8 Eg water vapour (3)
9 Towards a higher place (6)
10 Eg perform karaoke (4)
11 Exams (5)
13 Tiny sum of money (7)
15 Terse (7)
17 In the middle of (5)
21 Rebuff (4)
22 Fanciful; delightful (6)
23 Particle that is electrically charged (3)
24 Passageway (8)
25 Small houses (6)

Down

1 Persuasive and logical (6)
2 Important topics for debate (6)
3 ___ Newton: English physicist (5)
4 Dithers (7)
5 Capital of Finland (8)
6 Is unable to (6)
12 Bothered (8)
14 Take a seat (3,4)
16 Historical records (6)
18 Eg using a towel (6)
19 Unspecified objects (6)
20 Precious stone (5)

135

No. 133

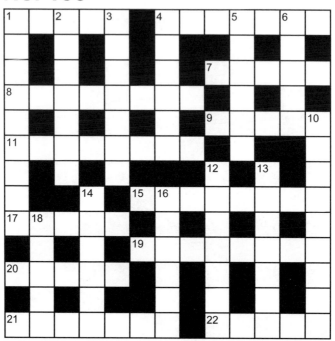

Across

1	Rustic (5)
4	Grouped together (7)
7	Lift up (5)
8	Unstable (8)
9	Toy bear (5)
11	Scottish seaport (8)
15	Peacemaker (8)
17	The spirit of a people (5)
19	Soldier (8)
20	Assumed appearance (5)
21	Water passage (7)
22	Judges (5)

Down

1	Respectable (9)
2	Male chicken (7)
3	Sweetened citrus beverage (7)
4	Caress (6)
5	Stopped (6)
6	Became less severe (5)
10	Almanacs (9)
12	Mythical female sea creature (7)
13	Unintelligent (7)
14	Child of your aunt or uncle (6)
16	Push forward (6)
18	Hard and durable (5)

No. 134

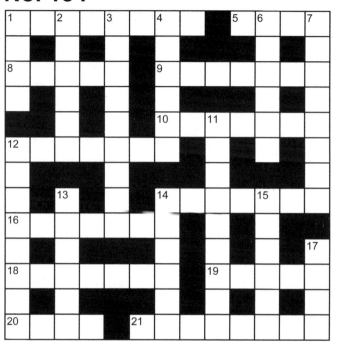

Across

1 Our flame (anag) (8)
5 Proofreader's mark (4)
8 Softly radiant (5)
9 Defensive wall (7)
10 Lie (7)
12 Scarf (7)
14 Smiled contemptuously (7)
16 Cunning (7)
18 Give reasons for (7)
19 Litre (anag) (5)
20 Mend with rows of stitches (4)
21 Naive or sentimental (4-4)

Down

1 Young horse (4)
2 Respite (6)
3 Reluctant (9)
4 Plant framework; bower (6)
6 Drinking vessel (6)
7 Note (4,4)
11 Communication between minds (9)
12 Squander money (8)
13 Aide (6)
14 Body position (6)
15 Repeat (6)
17 Network of lines (4)

CROSSWORD

SOLUTIONS

Solution 1

G	E	L	D	O	F		A		E		I	
A		I			A	C	R	I	M	O	N	Y
L	I	T			L		R		I		T	
E		M	U	E	S	L	I		S	T	E	W
N		U		E		V		S		N		
A	S	S	A	Y		D	E	F	A	C	T	O
		I		B		S		R				
T	E	A	R	F	U	L		H	Y	E	N	A
	N		B		L		S			Q		B
A	J	A	R		B	A	T	E	A	U		A
	O		U		O		U		P		A	P	T
D	Y	E	S	T	U	F	F			L		E
	S		H		S		F	L	A	S	K	S

Solution 2

S	C	A	R	C	E	L	Y		F	R	O	M
O		P		O	U				U			E
I	D	O	L	S		B	A	F	F	L	E	D
L		G		T		B			E			I
	E		A		E	N	G	O	R	G	E	
S	H	E	A	R	E	R		R		S		V
T			I			E						A
I		A		C		A	B	Y	S	S	A	L
M	U	S	T	A	N	G		H		T		
U		L			E		O		U		A	
L	E	E	R	Y	A	N		U	N	D	I	D
U		E			D		N		I			Z
S	A	P	S		H	A	N	D	S	O	M	E

Solution 3

C	U	B	E		C	O	L	L	E	C	T	S
A		A		A		R		A		U		A
P	A	C	I	F	I	C		B	E	L	O	W
A		O		F				O		P		S
C	O	N	T	E	M	P	O	R	A	R	Y	
I			C		L		A		I		N	
T	I	P		T	R	U	S	T		T	A	U
Y		A		I		M		O				M
	I	N	C	O	M	P	A	R	A	B	L	E
E		C		N			I		A		R	
P	L	A	Z	A		C	H	E	E	R	I	O
E		K		T		A		S		G		U
E	L	E	M	E	N	T	S		R	E	D	S

Solution 4

S	C	R	A	P	E		O	B	J	E	C	T
U		E		I		C		O		V		I
P	L	A	C	E	B	O		M		I		S
P		C		C		N	I	B	B	L	E	S
L	A	T	T	E		S		A				U
Y		I				T		R	H	Y	M	E
		O		B	A	R	E	D		I		
R	O	N	D	O		U			E			G
U				O		C		S	A	L	S	A
B	A	B	Y	S	I	T		C		D		R
R		L		T		E	L	U	S	I	O	N
I		O		E	D		B		N			E
C	I	C	A	D	A		H	A	N	G	A	R

Solution 5

L	E	P	O	R	I	N	E		A	R	E	A
E		L		E		U				O		B
A	X	I	O	M		A	S	S	A	Y	E	R
F		N		A		N			A		A	
		T		I		C	U	D	D	L	E	S
E	N	H	A	N	C	E		E		E		I
X				I				A				V
I		K		N		S	I	T	U	A	T	E
S	H	I	N	G	L	E		H		G		
T		M				N		T		O		C
I	V	O	R	I	E	S		R	O	U	G	H
N		N				E		A		T		U
G	R	O	W		A	D	O	P	T	I	N	G

Solution 6

D	A	R	E		E	M	B	A	T	T	L	E
A		O		M		E		B		R		A
T	O	M	B	O	L	A		S	E	A	T	S
A		E		T		G		E		V		E
B	R	O	T	H	E	R	I	N	L	A	W	
A				E		E		T		I		C
S	A	L	A	R	Y		I	M	E	L	D	A
E		I		T		E		I				P
	I	N	C	O	N	V	E	N	I	E	N	T
S		S		N		A		D		A		U
C	L	E	G	G		D	R	E	S	S	E	R
A		E		U		E		D		E		E
R	E	D	H	E	A	D	S		G	L	A	D

138

SOLUTIONS

Solution 7

A	I	D	S		S	I	M	U	L	A	T	E
R		R	S	C		N		C		V		
G	R	O	U	C	H	Y		F	O	R	T	E
U		O	H		L		Y		R		
A	P	P	R	O	A	C	H	A	B	L	E	
B			O	H		T		I		H
L	A	P		L	E	A	S	T		C	H	I
Y		E	M		R		E			G
	B	R	E	A	K	T	H	R	O	U	G	H
A		F	S			I		N		S
C	R	O	F	T		M	A	N	A	T	E	E
I		R	E		I		G		I		A
D	E	M	E	R	A	R	A		A	L	E	S

Solution 8

V	I	T	R	E	O	U	S		J	A	V	A
I		O		G		N			G		Q
N	E	W	L	Y		C	H	A	T	E	A	U
E		E	P		L			N		E
		R		T		O	M	I	T	T	E	D
T	O	S	S	I	N	G		N		S		U
O			A			C			C
M	S	N		T	R	A	N	S	I	T
A	R	T	I	S	T	S		P		A
H		O		E		A		F		I
A	P	R	I	C	O	T		B	E	A	S	T
W	E			S		L		R		C
K	E	Y	S		F	E	V	E	R	I	S	H

Solution 9

U	R	G	E		C	O	N	T	E	S	T	S
N		R		U		R		O		T		H
A	L	I	G	N	E	D		T	E	R	R	A
D		E	A		E		A		I		M
U	N	F	I	T		R	E	L	A	P	S	E
L			T		S		I		E		L
T	H	R	E	A	D		S	T	O	D	G	E
E		E		I		B		A			S
R	E	C	E	N	C	Y		R	A	I	L	S
A		O		A		L		I		R		N
T	H	U	M	B		I	M	A	G	I	N	E
E		N		L		N		N		S		S
D	I	T	H	E	R	E	D		W	H	Y	S

Solution 10

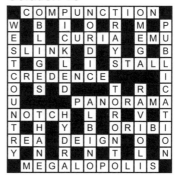

	C	O	M	P	U	N	C	T	I	O	N	
W		B		I		O		R		M		P
E	L		C	U	R	I	A		E	M	U	
S	L	I	N	K		D		Y		G		B
T		G		L		I		S	T	A	L	L
C	R	E	D	E	N	C	E					I
O		S		D			T		R		C
U			P	A	N	O	R	A	M	A	
N	O	T	C	H		L		R		V		T
T		H		Y		B		O	R	I	B	I
R	E	A		D	E	I	G	N		O		O
Y		N		R		N		T		L		N
	M	E	G	A	L	O	P	O	L	I	S	

Solution 11

R	O	T	O	R	S		S		G		M	
H		R		T	E	C	T	O	N	I	C	
Y	O	U		I		U		V		N
M		M	I	F	F	E	D		E	T	C	H
E		P		F		D		R		E
D	U	S	T	Y		W	E	T	N	E	S	S
			A		C		D		O
N	E	T	B	A	L	L		C	R	A	F	T
	N		L		A		D			C		A
S	T	Y	E		I	T	A	L	I	C		P
	R		T		M		I			E	K	E
M	A	Y	O	R	E	S	S			P		R
	P		P		D		Y	O	U	T	H	S

Solution 12

	S	I	S	T	E	R	I	N	L	A	W	
A		N		O		O		O		B		I
T		A		P	L	U	M	B		Y	E	N
M	E	N	U	S		N		L		S		H
O		E		P		D		E	N	S	U	E
S	I	L	L	I	E	S	T					R
P		Y		N			C		R		I
H					O	P	P	O	N	E	N	T
E	N	J	O	Y		E		N		D		A
R		O		O		N		G	R	O	A	N
I	N	K		U	N	T	I	E		I		C
C		E		T		U		A		N		E
	A	R	C	H	I	P	E	L	A	G	O	

139

SOLUTIONS

Solution 13

Solution 14

Solution 15

Solution 16

Solution 17

Solution 18

SOLUTIONS

Solution 19

Solution 20

Solution 21

Solution 22

Solution 23

Solution 24

CROSSWORD

SOLUTIONS

Solution 25

Solution 26

Solution 27

Solution 28

Solution 29

Solution 30

142

SOLUTIONS

CROSSWORD

Solution 31

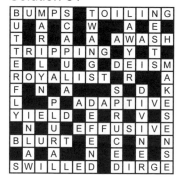

Solution 32

Solution 33

Solution 34

Solution 35

Solution 36

143

CROSSWORD

SOLUTIONS

Solution 37

Solution 38

Solution 39

Solution 40

Solution 41

Solution 42

144

SOLUTIONS

Solution 43

Solution 44

Solution 45

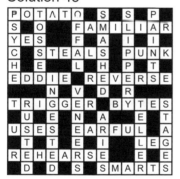

Solution 46

Solution 47

Solution 48

SOLUTIONS

CROSSWORD

Solution 49

```
S I T S . P O T A T O E S
C H . C . S . M . R . K
O V E R L A P . B U L K Y
O . T . O . R . I . A . E
T R A N S C E N D E N T .
E . . E . Y . E D . D . N
R A T I F Y . E X P O S E
S . R . I . R . T . . E
. B A T T L E G R O U N D
F . N . T . A . O . M . L
R I C C I . G R U M B L E
E . H . N . A . S . R . S
E M E R G I N G . C A B S
```

Solution 50

```
S I F T . U N W A S H E D
I . A . A . E . P . A . I
L E G I B L E . P U L P S
V . I . S . S . R . O . T
E O N . O . O . E D G E R
R . . L U N C H . E . U .
T . D U . . E . N . S .
O . E . T R A I N . . T
N O V A E . R . S . O A F
G . I . Z . C . I . Z . U
U N C L E . A X O L O T L
E . E . R . N . N . N . L
D I S P O S E D . D E F Y
```

Solution 51

```
M U S C U L A R . S T I R
A . E . N . R . A . O . E
L A T E R . T . R E N T S
I . T . E . E . T . E . I
. . F A I R M I N D E D .
S . S . S . Y . S . E . I
C O U P O N . A T T A I N
R . P . N . G . I . F . G
A P P E A R A N C E .
M . O . B . Z . A . P . S
B A S I L . E . L E I G H
L . E . E . B . L . L . O
E N D S . P O L Y G L O T
```

Solution 52

```
F I S T S . P R I M A T E
A . C . C . A . I . W .
N R . U . R . O S I E R
T R E A T I S E . L . E
A . E . T . O . D A N D Y
S I D E L I N E . Y . E
T . S . E . . H . I . A
I . N . A S S E S S O R
C R U E T . H . I . O . N
. A . V . C O N F E T T I
D I V A N . W . E . O . N
. D . D . E . R . P . G
E S C A P E D . S E E R S
```

Solution 53

```
H U S H U P . S . C . S
E . I . . E U P H O R I A
R U T . E . I . N . M
D . C H O P I N . T A I L
E . O . S . N . R . A
D A M E S . R E S I G N S
. . S . E . Y . V
A B S C O N D . M E D I C
. E . A . D . E . A . A
W H I P . G A R I S H . D
E . I . A . A . . L I D
T S U N A M I S . . I . I
. T . G . E . E X H A L E
```

Solution 54

```
I N C I T E . S T E P U P
N . H . O . A . R . U . A
S W E E T E N . I . F . E
I . E . E . T A C T F U L
S C R U M . E . K . . L
T . F . . C . L U C C A
. . U . O C H R E . H
L I L A C . A . . I . C
I . . C . M . V O L G A
S U C C U M B . E . D . E
T . A . L . E N E M I E S
E . T . T . R . R . S . A
D I S U S E . E S T H E R
```

146

SOLUTIONS

Solution 55

Solution 56

Solution 57

Solution 58

Solution 59

Solution 60

SOLUTIONS

Solution 61

A	M	B	L	E	R		R	E		A
N		O			O	V	E	R	T	A	K	E
N	I	T		G		S		C		I
O		T	H	R	U	S	H		H	E	M	S
Y		O		E		A		I		B
S	A	M	B	A		O	P	I	N	I	O	N
	E		E		E		G		
F	L	O	W	E	R	Y		A	S	K	E	D
	E		I		R		S		I		E
D	A	H	L		A	N	T	H	E	R		G
	G		D		T		E		S	I	R
Q	U	I	E	T	U	D	E			C		E
	E		R		M		D	A	P	H	N	E

Solution 62

E	A	S	Y		T	H	E	A	T	R	E	S
F		C		C		O		R		E		I
F	U	R	I	O	U	S		C	I	V	I	L
E		A		R		T		H		I		V
R	I	P	E	N		E	V	I	L	E	Y	E
V			I		L		T		W		R
E	N	M	E	S	H		S	E	E	S	A	W
S		Y		H		C		C			E
C	A	L	Y	P	S	O		T	R	I	E	D
E		E		A		N		U		C		D
N	E	E	D	S		T	E	R	M	I	N	I
C		N		T		R		E		N		N
E	V	E	R	Y	D	A	Y		A	G	O	G

Solution 63

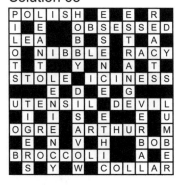

P	O	L	I	S	H		E		E		R
I		E			O	B	S	E	S	S	E	D
L	E	A		B		S		T		A
O		N	I	B	B	L	E		R	A	C	Y
T		T		Y		N		A		T
S	T	O	L	E		I	C	I	N	E	S	S
	E		D		E		G		
U	T	E	N	S	I	L		D	E	V	I	L
	I		I		S		E		E		U
O	G	R	E		A	R	T	H	U	R		M
	E		N		V		H		B	O	B
B	R	O	C	C	O	L	I			A		E
	S		Y		W		C	O	L	L	A	R

Solution 64

	D	I	S	C	O	U	R	T	E	S	Y
V		G		A		G		U		A		P
A		N		D	E	A	L	T		U	S	E
T	H	E	M	E		N		O		N		R
I		O		N		D		R	E	A	P	S
C	H	U	T	Z	P	A	H				O
A		S		A			P		N		N
N				P	A	R	A	B	O	L	A
C	A	S	E	D		T		C		T		L
I		T		U		R		K	H	A	K	I
T	W	O		C	H	I	N	A		B		T
Y		M		A		U		G		L		Y
	B	A	D	T	E	M	P	E	R	E	D

Solution 65

D	E	J	E	C	T	E	D		S	C	U	D
U		O		O		R		C		R		E
T	O	K	E	N		R		O	P	I	N	E
Y		E		S		O		I		T		P
			Q	U	A	R	A	N	T	I	N	E
D		O		L		S		C		C		N
I	M	P	U	T	E		V	I	V	A	C	E
S		T		A		V		D		L		D
M	A	I	N	T	A	I	N	E	D		
A		O		I		E		N		S		O
L	I	N	G	O		N		T	W	A	I	N
L		A		N		N		A		R		L
Y	O	L	K		F	A	U	L	T	I	L	Y

Solution 66

C	I	A	O		N	E	C	K	L	A	C	E
O		C		R		X		A		M		X
M	A	C	B	E	T	H		L	A	U	R	A
P		R		A		O		E		S		G
A	M	A	S	S		R	A	I	S	I	N	G
R			S		T		D		N		E
A	N	S	W	E	R		D	O	D	G	E	R
T		E		S		A		S			A
I	N	V	E	S	T	S		C	O	A	S	T
V		E		M		C		O		D		E
E	E	R	I	E		E	X	P	O	U	N	D
L		N		N		N		E		L		L
Y	U	L	E	T	I	D	E		S	T	A	Y

SOLUTIONS

Solution 67

F	E	S	T	E	R		S		E		R
E		T		U	N	T	E	S	T	E	D
D	O	E		N		Y		S		M	
O		R	A	D	I	A	L		A	G	A	R
R		E		N		I		Y		K	
A	L	O	H	A		A	S	P	I	R	E	S
		E		O		T		S			
U	S	E	L	E	S	S		S	T	O	K	E
	C		L		P		A		F		A
G	A	R	B		R	E	B	U	F	F		R
	T		E		E		D		I	N	N
T	H	A	N	K	Y	O	U		N		E
	E		T		S		L	E	D	G	E	R

Solution 68

S	T	E	E	R	A	G	E		B	A	S	H
O		N		E		L		T		E
M	A	G	I	C		A	N	D	R	O	I	D
E		I		O		N			M		G
		N		R		C	R	E	V	I	C	E
T	R	E	A	D	L	E		L		C		H
H		I					E			O
E		S		N		P	A	C	K	I	N	G
S	W	A	G	G	E	R		T		D
P		L		A		O		L		A
I	M	A	G	E	R	Y		R	U	I	N	S
A		M		E		A		N		H
N	A	I	L		P	R	O	L	O	G	U	E

Solution 69

E	E	L	S		E	S	P	O	U	S	A	L
A		I		E		I		V		T		O
R	E	M	O	V	E	S		E	X	A	M	S
L		I		O		K		R		R		S
I	N	T	E	L	L	I	G	I	B	L	E
E			U		N		N		E		A
S	A	L	U	T	E		E	D	I	T	E	D
T		O		I		A		U				D
	I	N	C	O	N	S	O	L	A	B	L	E
C		G		N		S		G		U		N
L	I	B	Y	A		U	P	E	N	D	E	D
A		O		R		R		D		G		U
N	E	W	L	Y	W	E	D		G	E	R	M

Solution 70

	A	F	F	I	R	M	A	T	I	O	N
C		E		N		E		E		N		A
H		S		M	I	N	I	M		S	I	T
E	X	T	R	A		T		P		E	T
E		O		T		A		T	I	T	H	E
S	L	O	V	E	N	L	Y				S
E		N		S			U		O		T
C				N	E	B	R	A	S	K	A
L	E	T	U	P		C		C		S		T
O		I		I		L		H	E	I	D	I
T	U	B		Q	U	A	S	I		C		O
H		I		U		I		N		L		N
	G	A	T	E	C	R	A	S	H	E	R

Solution 71

S	I	D	E	D		S	A	F	F	R	O	N
W		I		E		M		A		W	
A		V		M		I		S	T	I	N	G
L	A	U	R	E	A	T	E		H		E
L		L		S		E		M	E	T	R	E
O	R	G	A	N	I	S	T		R		L
W		E					L		S		U
E			A		G	I	G	A	N	T	I	C
D	O	D	G	Y		G		N		U		I
	B		E		A	L	L	O	T	T	E	D
S	A	I	N	T		O		L		T		A
	M		C		O		I		E	T	
S	A	W	Y	E	R	S		N	O	R	S	E

Solution 72

B	I	N	S		S	T	A	L	L	I	O	N
U		A		A		H		A		M		U
S	E	C	L	U	D	E		I	N	P	U	T
Y		H		T		L		S		E		S
B	I	O	C	H	E	M	I	S	T	R	Y
O			E		A		E		I		L
D	E	C	E	N	T		A	Z	A	L	E	A
Y		L		T		D		F				D
	L	E	G	I	T	I	M	A	T	E	L	Y
A		A		C		S		I		V		B
P	A	R	K	A		M	A	R	C	O	N	I
E		E		T		A		E		K		R
S	U	D	D	E	N	L	Y		D	E	E	D

149

CROSSWORD

SOLUTIONS

Solution 73

```
D O L T █ E M I N E N C E
I █ L █ O █ O █ U █ █ █ N
S T A F F E D █ N E P A L
P █ M █ I █ F █ T █ █ █ I
A G A P E █ F I L M I N G
S █ █ R █ Y █ A █ A █ █ H
S W E R V E █ A M U L E T
I █ L █ E █ B █ M █ █ █ E
O D Y S S E Y █ A P R O N
N █ S █ C █ E █ B █ A █ M
A F I R E █ B A L A N C E
T █ U █ N █ Y █ E █ C █ N
E N M I T I E S █ C H A T
```

Solution 74

```
A L B U M █ R O U T I N E
L █ O █ I █ E █ S █ O █ █
L A R P █ █ T H R O W █ █
O U T C R I E S █ I █ S █
T █ I █ O █ A █ D R I E S
T E N D R I L S █ T █ █ I
I █ G █ S █ █ A █ C █ D █
N █ O █ S C H E D U L E █
G N A S H █ H █ R █ R █ L
O █ T █ K A L A H A R I █
P I L L S █ L █ T █ T █ N
S █ E █ █ E █ E █ E █ E █
H Y D R A N T █ D I S C S
```

Solution 75

```
C U B A █ P H E A S A N T
I █ E █ H █ I █ L █ I █ R
R U I N O U S █ P O L K A
C █ N █ U █ S █ H █ M █ N
U R G E S █ E R A S E R S
M █ █ E █ S █ N █ N █ █ G
F A L L O W █ M U T T E R
E █ A █ F █ D █ M █ █ █ E
R E S O L V E █ E N N I S
E █ A █ O █ A █ R █ A █ S
N I G E R █ C H I A N T I
C █ N █ D █ O █ C █ N █ O
E V E N S O N G █ R Y A N
```

Solution 76

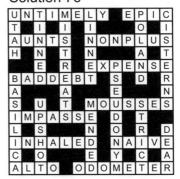

```
U N T I M E L Y █ E P I C
T █ I █ I █ I █ █ O █ █ I
A U N T S █ N O N P L U S
H █ N █ T █ N █ █ A █ █ T
█ █ E █ R █ E X P E N S E
B A D D E B T █ S █ D █ R
A █ █ A █ █ █ E █ █ E █ N
S █ U █ T █ M O U S S E S
I M P A S S E █ D █ T █ █
L █ S █ █ N █ O █ R █ D █
I N H A L E D █ N A I V E
C █ O █ █ E █ Y █ C █ A █
A L T O █ O D O M E T E R
```

Solution 77

```
S C R A M █ V I N T A G E
P █ U █ A █ A █ H █ A █ █
I █ S █ C █ L █ C R U S H
R U S H H O U R █ O █ E █
I █ I █ E █ E █ T W I S T
T R A I T O R S █ N █ H █
U █ N █ E █ █ █ T █ P █ R
A █ █ E █ O B D U R A T E
L I E N S █ O █ B █ T █ A
█ █ N █ E █ A R G U M E N T
P U R R S █ I █ L █ L █ E
█ R █ G █ █ N █ A █ L █ N
L E V Y I N G █ R E A R S
```

Solution 78

```
V I C E █ P O W E R F U L
E █ R █ S █ U █ X █ O █ E
H A I R C U T █ A G R E E
I █ E █ R █ █ G █ E █ K █
C A R D I O L O G I S T █
L █ P █ E █ E █ E █ E █ S
E N D █ T I M E R █ E A U
S █ I █ W █ M █ A █ █ █ B
█ O V E R C A U T I O U S
A █ I █ I █ █ █ I █ R █ I
C A D E T █ P R O D D E D
N █ E █ E █ E █ N █ E █ E
E N D U R I N G █ A R I D
```

SOLUTIONS

Solution 79

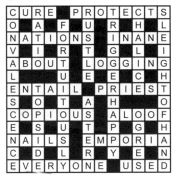

Solution 80

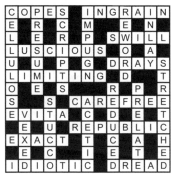

Solution 81

Solution 82

Solution 83

Solution 84

CROSSWORD

SOLUTIONS

Solution 85

Solution 86

Solution 87

Solution 88

Solution 89

Solution 90

SOLUTIONS

Solution 91

Solution 92

Solution 93

Solution 94

Solution 95

Solution 96

SOLUTIONS

Solution 97

```
F A T H E R L Y . . F I R M
L O . T . A . . . M . . I
A B B E Y . D E A D P A N
G . A . M . I . . A . . I
. G . O . N U A N C E S .
B O O T L E G . B . T . T
R . . O . . . Y . . R
O . F . G . E C S T A S Y
A L L O Y E D . M . D
D . O . . I . A . J . O
W O R N O U T . L A U G H
A . A . . O . L . R . M
Y U L E . G R E Y N E S S
```

Solution 98

Solution 99

```
A D D L E S . G L O B A L
S O . V . S . I . U . Y
P O W D E R Y . A . L . N
I . N . N . M A I L B O X
R U F F S . P . S . . E
E . A . . A . O A T H S
. . L . B A T O N . E
H A L V E . H . . E . D
O . . W . E . B A T H E
P R E D I C T . O . O . A
I . N . T . I G N I T E D
N . V . C . C . G . A . E
G L Y P H S . P O L L E N
```

Solution 100

Solution 101

Solution 102

SOLUTIONS

CROSSWORD

Solution 103

```
R O B I N S _ A F R E S H
E U O A A A A
B A T H T U B R R N
O T E S T A L L E D
R E E F S T W E
N R R A P P A L
U C R A Z Y A
R E P A Y C L A
E A T P I P E S
M A G E N T A O A S
O L I R I S I B L E
T U D T T L T
E L E V E N A S S E S S
```

Solution 104

```
S E T S _ C H A I R M A N
N R H E N I O
U N I C O R N C O N E S
G E P R O I E
N U R S E R Y R H Y M E
E L V E U E
S A S H E S P R I M A L
S Y S G E E
C R A S H L A N D I N G
B I N O T T A
O V A T E V I L L A I N
A N S E Y L C
R E A S S E S S B Y T E
```

Solution 105

```
D I V E S T F E A S T S
E I I A N E N
P A R S N I P G E I
O T K P L U M M E T
T R U S S R L C
S O O F I F T H
S G N A T S U
A D O R E C N N
T L H F U N G I
T S U N A M I O I G
I G T N E S T E G G
C L I G S S L
S P Y I N G S E T T E E
```

Solution 106

```
R E P L A C E M E N T
H N I H O O A
U S B R A W N O U R
M I N C E P T K M
A A R E H A S T E
N O R M A L L Y D
R E L S G F
I H I T H E R T O
G L E A M M O A R
H R E M C O M I C
T O O T R U N K M E
S D E N E A S
N E W S R E A D E R S
```

Solution 107

```
C A N E P R E S E N T S
O A D E H O I
U N D R E S S A B U Z Z
S A L O R V E
C A L L I G R A P H E R
O C T S A E
U P B E A T S H O U L D
S U T S O I
A F T E R T H O U G H T
C F S O T R I
E P I C S O R E G A N O
D N E L R N N
E D G I N E S S O D E S
```

Solution 108

```
C A M P P L A S T I C S
H Y C A U G P
A I R S H I P B I N G O
R R I D C O N
A S H R O O R B I T
C O R G A N L A
T A P S E N
E V R E L I C E
R I O J A I A G O
L C C C O M U
E N A C T A M U L E T S
S D O L S N L
S C O U R G E D E D G Y
```

SOLUTIONS

CROSSWORD

Solution 109

Solution 110

Solution 111

Solution 112

Solution 113

Solution 114

SOLUTIONS

Solution 115

Solution 116

Solution 117

Solution 118

Solution 119

Solution 120

CROSSWORD

SOLUTIONS

Solution 121

Solution 122

Solution 123

Solution 124

Solution 125

Solution 126

158

SOLUTIONS

Solution 127

Solution 128

Solution 129

Solution 130

Solution 131

Solution 132

SOLUTIONS

Solution 133

R	U	R	A	L		F	L	O	C	K	E	D
E		O		I		O		E		A		
P		O		M		N		R	A	I	S	E
U	N	S	T	E	A	D	Y		S		E	
T		T		A		L		T	E	D	D	Y
A	B	E	R	D	E	E	N		D			E
B		R		E				M		A		A
L			C		A	P	P	E	A	S	E	R
E	T	H	O	S		R		R		I		B
	O		U		C	O	M	M	A	N	D	O
G	U	I	S	E		P		A		I		O
	G		I		E		I		N		K	
C	H	A	N	N	E	L		D	E	E	M	S

Solution 134

F	O	R	M	U	L	A	E		S	T	E	T
O		E		N		R			E			A
A	G	L	O	W		B	U	L	W	A	R	K
L		I		I		O			C			E
	E		L		U	N	T	R	U	T	H	
M	U	F	F	L	E	R		E		P		E
I			I				L			L		E
S		H		N		S	N	E	E	R	E	D
S	L	E	I	G	H	T		P		E		
P		L		A		A		A		P		G
E	X	P	L	A	I	N		T	I	L	E	R
N		E		C		H		H		A		I
D	A	R	N		D	E	W	Y	E	Y	E	D